W9-CMP-972

The Ancient Olympic Games

The Ancient Olympic Games

Judith Swaddling

LUTHER L. GOBBEL LIBRARY
LAMBUTH COLLEGE
JACKSON, TENNESSEE
WITHDRAWN

102887

University of Texas Press, Austin

Published in co-operation with the British Museum

International Standard Book Number
0-292-70373-2
Library of Congress Catalog Card Number
83-51502
Copyright © 1980 by The Trustees of the
British Museum
All rights reserved
First University of Texas Press Edition, 1984

Designed by James Shurmer

Set in Monophoto Bembo (270) by
Filmtype Services Limited, Scarborough and
printed in England by Pindar Print Limited,
Scarborough, North Yorkshire

Frontispiece: Herakles, founder of the Olympic
Games, is received into heaven. A winged figure
of Victory presents him with a garland, and the
god Zeus looks on, bearing his winged
thunderbolt and sceptre. Herakles has his
traditional attributes: a club, bow and lionskin.
From an amphora made in Athens *c.*475–450 BC.
BMC Vases E 262.

Front cover: Marble statue of a discus-thrower
(see p.51).

Back cover: Entrance tunnel to the stadium, with
the bases of the Zanes (see p.41).

Acknowledgments

I should like to acknowledge with thanks the co-
operation and assistance of Dr Mallwitz and Dr
Schilbach of the *Deutsches Archäologisches Institut*,
currently working on the Olympia excavations,
Kim Allen and his team of model-makers, Sue
Bird who did the drawings and Robert
Broomfield who provided the photographs of
the site.

The model of Olympia was specially
commissioned by the Trustees of the British
Museum for the Exhibition 'The Ancient
Olympic Games'.
All the objects illustrated are in the collections of
the British Museum. The objects are referred to
either by the catalogue number (BMC = British
Museum Catalogue) or by their registration
number.

GV23
.S9
1980

Contents

'*There are enough irksome and troublesome things in life; aren't things just as bad at the Olympic festival? Aren't you scorched there by the fierce heat? Aren't you crushed in the crowd? Isn't it difficult to freshen yourself up? Doesn't the rain soak you to the skin? Aren't you bothered by the noise, the din and other nuisances? But it seems to me that you are well able to bear and indeed gladly endure all this, when you think of the gripping spectacles that you will see.*'

Epictetus, first–second century AD,
Dissertations I 6. 23–9

1 The Olympic Games: where and why?

Every fourth year for a thousand years, from 776 BC to AD 395, the pageantry of the Olympic festival attracted citizens from all over the Greek world. They flocked to Olympia, the permanent setting for the Games, in the early years coming in their hundreds from neighbouring towns and city-states, and later in their thousands by land and sea from colonies as far away as Spain and Africa. What drew them all this way to endure the discomforts which Epictetus records? The Games, of course, and perhaps no less the celebratory banquets that followed, but there was something more. . .

The Games were held in honour of the god Zeus, the supreme god of Greek mythology, and a visit to Olympia was also a pilgrimage to his most sacred place, the grove known as the Altis. There is no modern parallel for Olympia; it would have to be a site combining a sports complex and a centre for religious devotion, something like a combination of Wembley Stadium and Westminster Abbey.

Olympia is situated in a fertile, grassy plain on the north bank of the broad river Alpheios, just to the east of its confluence with the Kladeos, which rushes down to meet it from the mountains of Elis. In ancient times the area was pleasantly shaded with plane and olive-trees, white poplars and even palm-trees, while vines and flowering shrubs grew thickly beneath them. Rising above the site, to the north, is the lofty, pine-covered hill of Kronos, named after the father of Zeus. Successive waves of peoples who passed through the area in prehistoric times each observed the sanctity of this hallowed area. Modern visitors to the site often express surprise that the Games were held in such a remote area, but in antiquity , the river Alpheios was navigable, and Olympia was easily accessible both from the sea (it was about fifteen kilometres from the coast) and by means of inland routes converging on the site. The hill of Kronos (Plan 35) must always have been a conspicuous landmark in the surrounding terrain.

The clearing within the grove at the foot of the hill was once associated with fertility rites, for here was a very ancient oracle of Ge, the earth goddess. Gradually, as the worship of Zeus became predominant, people began to honour him at simple altars in the grove and hung their offerings – primitive terracotta and bronze figurines of men and animals – on the branches of nearby trees. With the establishment of the Games, this sanctuary grew and flourished. From the sixth century BC onwards the Altis was gradually adorned with temples, treasuries, halls, elaborate altars and literally hundreds of marble and bronze statues. The statues, some of which were several times life-size, were mostly victory dedications to Zeus for athletic and military achievements, and were set up by both states and individuals. There were also monuments erected in honour of benefactors, and offerings of costly materials given by wealthy tyrants and princes. Most remarkable of all the spectacles at Olympia was one of the 'Seven Wonders of the World': the

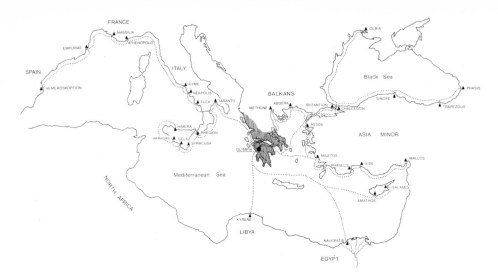

Athletes came from hundreds of miles away to take part in the Olympic Games. For many centuries only citizens of Greece were allowed to compete, and these are the Greek colonies from which competitors came in the fifth century BC.

The Olympic Games were held in honour of Zeus. Inside his temple at Olympia was a magnificent thirteen-metre-high, gold and ivory statue of the god. Although the statue was destroyed many centuries ago, its general appearance is known from contemporary descriptions and from representations on coins and small-scale copies. *(Right)* bronze statuette of Zeus, Roman, about second century AD. Height 18.4 cm.
BMC Bronzes 909.

resplendent thirteen-metre-high gold and ivory statue of Zeus within his magnificent temple. The statue was the work of Pheidias, the great sculptor of the fifth century BC.

As regards the origin of the Olympic Games, one can, as often in Greek history, either believe the legends, of which there are many, or look for a more down-to-earth beginning. According to the poet Pindar, Olympia was virtually created by Herakles, the 'superman' of Greek mythology. He made a clearing in the grove, laid out the boundaries of the Altis and instituted the first games in honour of Zeus. His purpose was to celebrate the success of one of his twelve labours, the cleaning of the cattle stables of King Augeas of Elis, which had been achieved by diverting the river Alpheios from its course. It is more likely, however, that athletic festivals like the Olympic Games developed from the funeral games which were held in honour of local heroes. Pelops, of whom we shall speak later, was the local hero of Olympia, and his grave and sanctuary were situated within the Altis. It is interesting that he was said to come from the east, for many people believe that it was in Asia Minor that the first organised athletic contests took place, when the Greek communities established there became prosperous enough to devote their leisure time to sport. At that time mainland Greece was still unsettled by wars and migrations.

The traditional date for the establishment of the Olympic Games was 776 BC, but competitions appear to have been held on an unofficial basis long before this. King Iphitos of Elis, a shadowy figure who lived around the ninth century BC, is said to have reinstituted the Games on the advice of the Delphic Oracle. The king had asked the Oracle how to bring an end to the civil wars and pestilence which were gradually destroying the land of Greece, whereupon the priestess advised that he should restore the Olympic Games and declare a truce for their duration. Whether this is true or not the Olympic Truce was a major instrument in the unification of the Greek states and colonies.

In order to spread the news of the Truce before the beginning of the Olympic festival, three heralds decked with olive wreaths and carrying staffs were sent out from Elis to every Greek state. It was the heralds' duty to announce the exact date of the festival, to invite the inhabitants to attend and, most important of all, to

(Right) Silver coin minted by the Eleans, who were the controllers of the Olympic festival, showing Zeus and a personification of Olympia 370–362 BC. Diameter 2.5 cm. BM Catalogue of Coins, Elis 72.

(Far right) The efficacy of the Sacred Truce depended largely upon the maintenance of neutrality by the Eleans, which was achieved in part by treaties established with other city-states. This bronze tablet records an alliance between the Eleans and the Heraians of Arcadia for one hundred years, and states that any offender against the agreement must pay one talent of silver to Zeus at Olympia. *c.* 500 BC, from Olympia. Height 10.2 cm. BMC Bronzes 264.

9

The model of Olympia, specially commissioned
by the Trustees of the British Museum for the exhibition
'The Ancient Olympic Games'. On a scale of 1:200, it
faithfully reproduces in miniature the buildings,
monuments and landscape as they would have appeared
c. 100 BC, before extensive building work and alterations

were carried out by the Romans. Although it is evident that in antiquity there were many hundreds of statues at Olympia, only a few of the principal ones have been included on the model, both for simplicity and because in the majority of cases neither the appearance nor the exact location is known.

announce the Olympic Truce. In this way they came to be known as the Truce-Bearers, *Spondophoroi*; they served not only as heralds but also as full-time legal advisers to the Eleans. Originally the Truce lasted for one month but it was extended to two and then three months, to protect visitors coming from further afield. The terms of the Truce were engraved on a bronze discus which was kept in the Temple of Hera in the Altis. It forbade states participating in the Games to take up arms, to pursue legal disputes or to carry out death penalties. This was to ensure that pilgrims and athletes travelling to and from Olympia would have a safe journey. Violators of the Truce were heavily fined, and indeed on one occasion, Alexander the Great himself had to recompense an Athenian who was robbed by some of his mercenaries whilst travelling to Olympia.

The Olympic Games are the oldest of the four panhellenic or national athletic festivals which composed the *periodos* or 'circuit' games. The other three were the Pythian Games at Delphi, held in honour of Apollo, the Isthmian Games held at Corinth for Poseidon, and the Games at Nemea, which, like the Olympics, were in honour of Zeus. A major distinction between the Greek games and our own is that all major and minor athletic festivals, of which several hundred had been established by Roman times, were celebrated under the patronage of a divinity. The god was believed to bestow on the athletes the physical prowess which enabled them to take part in the Games. Accordingly, the athletes prayed to the deity and promised offerings should they be victorious.

The Olympic festival was celebrated once every four years in accordance with the Greek calendar, which was based on the lunar month. It was always timed so that the central day of the festival coincided with the second or third full moon after the summer solstice. This may well indicate the assimilation at some stage of the Games with fertility rites which celebrated the harvesting. It is often asked why the Greeks should have chosen the very hottest time of the year, mid-August or mid-September, for such strenuous exertion. Apart from the lunar associations it surely made sense to hold the Games at the one time during the year when work on the land was at a standstill. By then the crops were gathered and there was a lull in which men were eager to relax and celebrate the end of a hard year's work.

The four major athletic festivals in Greece came to be known as the *periodos* or 'circuit'. Important games were also held at Athens as part of the Panathenaic festival, but this was a local event. Over the centuries hundreds of other city-states established their own games, many modelled on the Olympics; some of these even negotiated with the Eleans the right to entitle their games 'Olympic'.

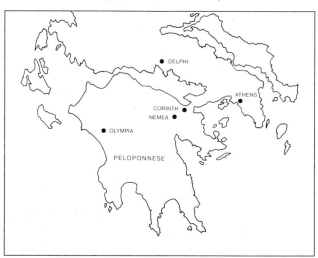

2 The Site

Our sources of knowledge for Olympia

If Olympia had not been rediscovered in 1766 by Richard Chandler, an English antiquarian carrying out an exploratory mission on behalf of the Society of Dilettanti, it is likely that the Olympic Games as we know them might never have existed.

It is ironic that the site of Olympia, which was chosen for its strategic position, should be destroyed by natural forces peculiar to the locality. In the fourth century AD two massive earthquakes tore the sanctuary apart, toppling the columns and shattering the walls of the most hallowed precinct of antiquity. In the west the river Kladeos burst its banks, destroying almost half the gymnasium, and never returning to its former course. Winter storms deposited rocks and earth from the nearby hill of Kronos over the area, and in the late Middle Ages the river Alpheios, flowing in the south, also flooded the sanctuary, washing away the hippodrome. As a result the entire site was covered with silt to an average depth of four metres, and the location of the sanctuary became forgotten.

Fourteen hundred years later, in 1829, a French team of archaeologists investigated the site, but it was not until 1875 that full-scale excavations were carried out by the German government, with the consent of the Greek authorities. The newly enthroned Kaiser Wilhelm I had been entranced by the vision of Olympia ever since hearing a lecture by Professor Ernst Curtius at the University of Berlin in 1852. The subsequent excavations, which lasted six years, took place under the direction of this eminent archaeologist. With characteristic speed and efficiency the Germans regularly published the results of their findings.

The reports fired the imagination of Pierre de Coubertin, a French nobleman, who became obsessed with the athletic ideal of Olympia. Saddened by the low

The areas south and west of Olympia were prone to frequent flooding from the rivers Kladeos and Alpheios which converged nearby. Earthquakes in the fourth century AD, followed by floods, devastated the sanctuary and left it covered by several metres of silt.

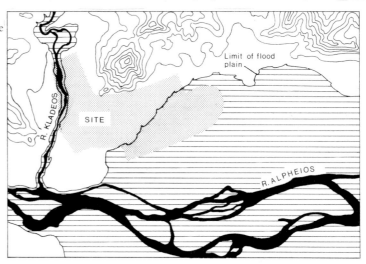

(*Right*) The artist Sir William Gell, travelling companion of Edward Dodwell, the archaeologist (seated right foreground), sketched the countryside around Olympia in 1806. Though the hill of Kronos is conspicuous to the left in the distance, there is scarcely any indication of the sanctuary itself, lying below it to the right, still deep under the silt.

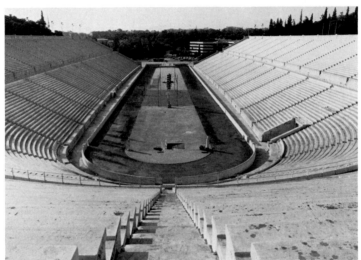

(*Right, below*) The marble stadium at Athens, reconstructed for the staging of the first modern Olympic Games in 1896.

morale of the French people since the defeat of Napoleon, Baron de Coubertin resolved to rekindle the competitive flame of the ancient Olympic Games. Largely due to his inspired efforts the first modern Olympic Games were held in Athens in 1896, where a magnificent marble stadium had been reconstructed for the occasion. Coubertin believed that the Olympic ideal would inspire amongst nations a competitiveness and team spirit unknown to the modern world. In fact the Greek ideal had been the physical excellence of the individual rather than the state, and the celebration of this gift in honour of the god.

In 1936 the German Institute of Archaeology began systematic excavation of the site and to this day they are continuing to reveal the reality of the myth.

Religious and civic monuments

1 Great Altar of Zeus

The altar is believed to have existed as early as the tenth century BC. According to legend it marked the spot struck by a thunderbolt which Zeus hurled from his throne on Mount Olympos, when he laid claim to the area as his sacred precinct. In Pausanias' time the altar consisted of a stone base surmounted by a conical pile of ashes, seven metres high, accumulated from sacrifices made to Zeus. The ashes left from each sacrifice were mixed with water from the Alpheios. The resulting paste was then plastered on to the altar, and subsequently solidified, year by year increasing the overall height. Ash from sacrifices made on the altar of Hestia in the Prytaneion was also added to the mound.

A reconstruction of the Great Altar of Zeus, where one hundred oxen, a gift from the people of Elis, were sacrificed to Zeus on the middle day of the Olympic Festival.

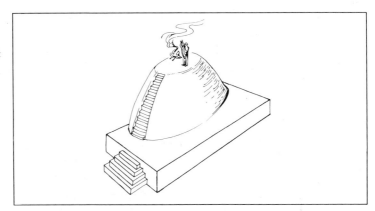

2 Temple of Zeus

This magnificent temple took ten years to build and was completed in 456 BC. It was financed by spoils taken by the Eleans from neighbouring tribes, who were predominantly worshippers of Hera, and initially resisted the establishment of Zeus as the supreme deity.

The temple was designed by an architect named Libon, who came from Elis. It must have been a remarkable sight: there were thirty-four massive columns, surmounted by mouldings painted with intricate patterns in glowing red, blue and

The model of the Temple of Zeus. The *akroteria*, the ornaments on the corners of the roof, are gilt bronze tripods and figures of Victory.
The sculpture in the pediments was originally painted, but as the colours are now lost they have not been included on the model.

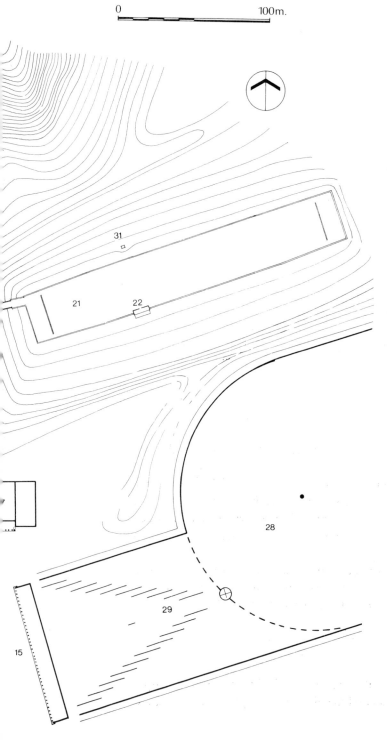

Plan of Olympia
*c.*100 BC

0 ————————————— 100m.

Key

1 Great Altar of Zeus
2 Temple of Zeus
3 Pheidias' workshop
4 Statue of Victory by Paionios
5 Sacred olive-tree
6 Temple of Hera
6a Altar of Hera
7 Temple of Meter
7a Altar of Meter
8 Pelopion
9 Philippaion
10 Prytaneion
11 Bouleuterion
12 Leonidaion
13 Echo Colonnade
14 Southern Colonnade
15 Colonnade of Agnaptos
16 South Eastern Colonnade
17 'Greek building'
18 Heroon
19 'Theokoleon'
20 Treasuries
21 Stadium
22 Judges' stand
23 Entrance tunnel to stadium
24 Gymnasium
25 Palaistra
26 Bathing facilities
27 Swimming pool
28 Hippodrome
29 Starting gate for horse-races
30 Zanes (statues of Zeus)
31 Altar of Demeter Chamyne
32 Pillar of Oinomaos
33 Altis wall
34 Retaining wall of river Kladeos
35 Hill of Kronos

gold. Over one hundred marble water-spouts in the form of lions' heads drained water from the roof, which was tiled entirely in Pentelic marble specially brought from the quarries near Athens. In later times twenty-one gilded shields, dedicated by the Roman general Mummius after he sacked Corinth in 144 BC, were hung above the columns.

Many fine sculptures adorned the temple. The pediments, or gables, depicted two legendary scenes: in the east, Zeus presided over the preparations for the chariot-race between Pelops and Oinomaos (see p.66). In the west a battle raged between two mythological tribes, the Lapiths and the Centaurs. Inside the porches, high up under the ceiling, were panels representing the twelve labours of Herakles, the legendary creator of the Olympic Games.

As with other Greek temples, it is difficult to establish exactly what took place inside. The temple itself was primarily a shelter for the cult statue of the god, rather than a place of worship. There were many other statues and offerings which must have given the interior the appearance of a museum. Entry to temples was often restricted to priests, but at Olympia, at least by the time of Pausanias, visitors were allowed inside to see the great statue of Zeus.

'The god is seated on a throne. He is made of gold and ivory, and on his head is a wreath representing sprays of olive. In his right hand stands a figure of Victory, also of gold and ivory...in his left hand is a sceptre, skilfully wrought from a variety of metals. The bird perched on the sceptre is an eagle. The sandals of the god are of gold, and so is his robe, which is decorated with animals and lilies. The throne is adorned with gold, precious stones, ebony and ivory; it is painted and carved with figures...I know that the measurements of height and breadth of Zeus at Olympia have been recorded, but I cannot commend the men who took the measurements, for their information falls far short of the impression which the image makes on the spectator.'

Pausanias, second century AD, *Description of Greece* V 11.1–2,9

This colossal figure, thirteen metres high, was considered one of the 'Seven Wonders of the World'. It required so much ivory that Philo of Byzantium claimed this statue by Pheidias to be the reason why nature had created elephants. The head was so near to the ceiling that critics jibed that if Zeus stood up, he would literally raise the roof.

Pheidias, who had already made the gold and ivory figure of Athena for the Parthenon in Athens, designed the statue and supervised its construction in his workshop west of the Altis. It was hollow, supported by an armature of wooden beams among which in later years, Lucian would have us believe, there lived a colony of rats and mice.

At the end of the fourth century AD the statue was looted and taken to a palace in Istanbul, so escaping the burning of the temple some thirty years later. But ironically it too was destroyed by a fire which razed many of the buildings in Istanbul in AD 462.

3 Pheidias' Workshop

This impressive studio was especially built to reproduce the interior of the Temple of Zeus, for it was here that Pheidias created the gold and ivory statue. During the

(Right) The chryselephantine (gold and ivory) statue of Zeus, which stood over thirteen metres high. Pausanias says that a spiral staircase to an upper floor in the aisles of the temple enabled visitors to take a closer look at the god.

(Far right) The Nike, or Victory, of Paionios, which stood before the temple of Zeus: the reconstruction of the figure is based on the damaged though impressive remains, now in the Olympia Museum.

excavations various tools, fragments of moulds for drapery, particles of gold, ivory, glass and semi-precious stones were found, together with a cup which has scratched on the bottom 'I belong to Pheidias'. In the fifth century AD the building was converted into a church.

4 Statue of Victory by Paionios

This striking figure of Victory swooping down from the heavens is one of the very few victory monuments to survive. Balanced on the back of an eagle in full flight, she was perched on top of a pillar nine metres high, which still stands before the Temple of Zeus. The figure was originally brightly painted; her drapery was red, and her hair black, bound by a gold ribbon. It was dedicated by the Messenians, who, with their allies the Athenians, gained a momentous victory over the Spartans in the 420s BC, bringing a temporary halt to the Peloponnesian War.

The statue was made by Paionios of Mende. In the inscription on the base, Paionios refers to his own victory in creating the *akroteria* (statues at each end of the roof) for the Temple of Zeus. This may refer to a competition for designs submitted

The temple of Hera today from the south east. In the foreground are remains belonging to the prehistoric settlement.

by various artists, a common practice in antiquity to decide who should receive a commission,

5 Sacred olive-tree from which the Olympic crowns were made (see p. 74).

6 and 6a Temple and altar of Hera

This was the first temple to be built in the Altis in around 600 BC, and, save for the foundations of the prehistoric settlement in the north of the site, it is the oldest building at Olympia of which any remains survive.

It was probably erected by local tribes who paid homage to Hera, before the Eleans established Zeus as the sovereign deity in the Altis. There were two cult images in the temple, one of Hera and one of Zeus, the combination of the two statues symbolising the union of religious beliefs between the two peoples. During excavations a female head of limestone, twice life-size, was found west of the temple, but it very likely belonged to a sphinx and not to the statue of Hera.

The most remarkable feature of the temple was that no two of the columns were exactly alike, differing in style, thickness and type of stone. It appears that originally all the columns were made of wood, and were replaced one by one in stone as, over the years, they gradually rotted. They were probably not all removed at once because it would be considered sacrilegious to remove any part of the temple unless absolutely essential. It is possible that each stone column was dedicated by a different person and this would account for the lack of uniformity. Originally only the foundations and lower parts of the walls were of stone; the upper walls were of mudbrick, and wooden rafters supported the terracotta roof-tiles.

7 and 7a Temple and altar of Meter

The goddess Meter, otherwise known as Rhea, was the mother of Zeus and wife of Kronos. The temple was built in the fourth century BC, and its alignment was unusual, for the main façade was in the west, rather than the east as in most Greek temples. This may have been because it was considered essential that the temple faced the sacred altar, and the ideal site to the west was already occupied by the Temple of Hera. The altar of Meter had been in use for several centuries before a temple to her was erected. Altars were almost always situated in the open air, and worshippers made sacrifices, usually under the supervision of a priest.

8 Pelopion

Within this walled area was the so-called burial mound of the hero Pelops. Excavations have revealed a number of graves but there is no evidence to suggest a major burial. The graves date back to the third millennium BC, but the wall and grand entrance porch were not erected until the fifth or fourth century BC. Pausanias records that a shoulder-blade, believed to be that of Pelops, had been found there.

9 Philippaion

This elegant building, roofed with carved marble tiles surmounted by a bronze poppy-head, was dedicated by Philip II of Macedon in celebration of both military and athletic victories. Philip had already won several chariot-races at Olympia, and his victory over the Greeks at Chaironeia in 338 BC presented the opportunity for a lavish dedication. He died only two years after the battle, and it is likely that his son Alexander the Great supervised the completion of the monument. Its circular shape is reminiscent of the beehive-tombs, called *tholoi*, which survive from the Mycenaean period. It may have been designed as a kind of cenotaph, especially as it housed statues depicting members of the Macedonian royal family. These were made from gold and ivory, materials normally reserved for images of the gods. The Altis wall (Plan 33) was laid out to incorporate the Philippaion within the sacred precinct, indicating the desire of the Macedonians to establish themselves as cult figures in the Greek world.

10 Prytaneion

The many fragments of bronze vessels found during the excavation of this building support Pausanias' statement that it was the location of the great banquet given for victors in the Games. It was also an administrative centre for the cult and the festival. Built around 470 BC, it is believed to have housed the sacred fire of Hestia, goddess of the hearth, which was kept burning day and night, and from which a flame was carried to light the fires on all the other altars in the sanctuary. The poor condition of the foundations and the successive phases of building on the site have made this the most difficult building to reconstruct of all those at Olympia.

11 Bouleuterion

The Bouleuterion, or Council-House, was an ancient and venerable conglomeration of buildings. The south wing was constructed first, in around 550 BC, then followed the north wing, the central chamber and finally the colonnade in the east. The apsidal shape of the wings was a traditional design, originating several centuries earlier. The Olympic council held their meetings here, and the archives were possibly kept in the semi-circular store-rooms at the end of each hall.

The statue of Zeus Horkios, in front of which Pausanias says the athletes, their

(*Left*) The north-western part of the Altis. To the right is the Temple of Hera; the decorative discs at each end of the roof are of terracotta, painted with intricate geometric designs in hues of brown and purple. On the left is the Pelopion, or burial mound of Pelops; in the time of Pausanias many statues stood among the trees in the enclosure. The circular building is the Philippaion, and beyond are the palaistra and the gymnasium.

(*Centre*) The Temple of Meter stands by the terrace wall, along which are placed the Zanes. Above is the row of Treasuries, five of which were set up by Greek colonies in Sicily and southern Italy (Selinus, Gela, Syrakuse, Metapontum and Sybaris), the others by Epidamnos in Illyria, Byzantium on the Black Sea, Kyrene in Northern Africa and Sikyon and Megara on the Greek mainland. Most were decorated with painted terracotta panels and roof ornaments.

(*Bottom*) In the foreground are the Southern Colonnade (*left*) and the Bouleuterion. Behind are two small buildings whose usage is uncertain, while further back is the Leonidaion, the largest single structure at Olympia.

relations and trainers swore the oath at the beginning of the festival, stood in the Bouleuterion, probably in the central room.

12 Leonidaion

This was an hotel for visiting officials and VIPs. It was built in the fourth century BC at the expense of a certain Leonidas of Naxos, after whom it was named. It comprised numerous guestrooms and apartments for visitors who could stroll in the outer colonnade, which ran right round the building, and the inner colonnade, which looked on to the courtyard. There were probably trees and flower-beds in the courtyard, but the Roman water-gardens have destroyed any evidence that may have existed for their layout.

13 Echo Colonnade

Constructed soon after the middle of the fourth century BC, the architectural style of the building strongly resembles that of the Philippaion and it has been suggested that Philip II dedicated both buildings. Situated along the eastern edge of the Altis, it formed a boundary which emphasised the separation of the stadium and hippodrome from the sanctuary.

Pausanias says that it was sometimes called the 'Painted Colonnade' because of the paintings on its walls. But it was usually known as the 'Echo Colonnade' as it echoed a man's voice seven times or more, and because of this the contests for heralds and trumpeters were held at the northern end. The narrow courtyard at the back was probably a store for athletic equipment.

14 Southern Colonnade

This elegant colonnade was built around 350 BC and would have provided a pleasant spot from which onlookers could watch the horses and chariots going to and from the hippodrome. At the start of the Games the *Hellanodikai*, or judges of the Games, may have provided an official welcome under the projecting porch for the procession coming along the Sacred Way from Elis.

15 Colonnade of Agnaptos

Although Pausanias mentions this building there is now no trace of it for any remains were swept away during the flood. Agnaptos constructed the building shortly after the Echo Colonnade was completed, and as it is believed to have stood at the back of the *aphesis* (the starting gate for horse-races) and at right angles to the Southern Colonnade, the space between the two colonnades probably served as an assembly area for horses and chariots.

16 South Eastern Colonnade

The purpose of this building, constructed around 375 BC, is uncertain, although it may have been the *Hellanodikaion*, or 'Judges' Building'. The judges had another building in Elis where they prepared for the Games.

17 'Greek Building'

The uninformative title given to this building indicates our lack of knowledge about it. In early times there may have been a sanctuary of the goddess Hestia on the site, but the buildings later constructed there seem to have housed workshops.

18 Heroon

This building is known as the 'Heroon', as an altar dedicated to an unknown hero was found within it. Originally, however, it was a bath-house (see p.30).

19 'Theokoleon'

This building, erected in the latter part of the fifth century BC, was for many years identified as the *theokoleon* or 'Priests' House', where various religious officials could hold their meetings. Pausanias, however, indicates that the Priests' House was in the north near the Prytaneion, and the true identification of this building remains uncertain. As it is next to Pheidias' workshop, it may have provided living quarters for craftsmen or served as a store for the precious materials which they used.

20 Treasuries

The row of treasuries, each resembling a minature temple, stood on a specially constructed terrace at the foot of the hill of Kronos (Plan 35). There were eleven in all; the smallest structure, fifth from the right, was an altar. Each was set up by a Greek colony, wishing to gain prestige in their homeland. They housed objects of value, particularly those which needed shelter from the weather, and deposits of money. Because of this, over the years Olympia came to be regarded as a kind of banking centre.

The ancient sports complex

21 Stadium

The stadium did not exist during the early years of the Olympic Games. The athletes made use of an open level stretch of ground with a line drawn in the sand to mark the start (giving rise to our term 'starting from scratch'). As the races were held in honour of the god Zeus, it was appropriate that the finishing line should be close to his altar. The spectators stood on the lower slopes of the hill of Kronos.

These simple arrangements were adequate for the first centuries of the Olympic Games. Gradually various improvements were made and a rudimentary stadium was constructed within the Altis. It had shallow banks and a rectangular track, for, unlike ours, all ancient races were run on the straight. Eventually, around 350 BC a magnificent new stadium was constructed and it was situated, significantly, outside the Altis boundaries. By this time the games, although still part of the religious festival, had become established in their own right. Originally Zeus had been glorified for granting powers of strength and physical endurance to the athletes; now the athletes were becoming increasingly professional and beginning to gain recognition as cult figures themselves. Thus the removal of the stadium from the sacred precinct was a development in religious as well as athletic history.

View of the stadium from the east, with the remains of the entrance tunnel at the far end.
The slopes of the pine-clad hill of Kronos have subsided since antiquity, giving it a gentler less dramatic appearance.

The track in the stadium was of clay, levelled and lightly covered with sand. It had stone sills towards each end which marked the start and finish of the races (see p.46). To preserve some of the religious significance of the games it was desirable for all races to finish at the western end of the course, so that the runners still ran towards the heart of the Altis as they had done in the early days. Races consisting of an even number of lengths were therefore started at the western end. The course was separated from the embankment by a ridge of stone blocks, to the outside of which was a channel that conducted water round the stadium, discharging at intervals into basins for the refreshment of spectators who stood all day in the blazing sun without any shelter.

The length of the track at Olympia is six hundred Olympic feet, 192.27 metres. According to mythology, Herakles fixed the distance of the original race (and ultimately of the stadium) by placing one foot in front of the other six hundred times. An alternative explanation was that Herakles was able to run this distance in one breath before pausing to take another. Thus it has been suggested that 'stadium' was derived from the Greek word 'to stand.' All ancient stadia were approximately six hundred feet in length but most places used a local standard of measure, causing a slight variation in the length of each stadium.

The ground rose naturally in the east and artificial embankments were constructed in the north, west and south, requiring an immense amount of labour. In this way a surprising total of between forty and forty-five thousand spectators could be accommodated. To afford spectators an uninterrupted view of the race the two long embankments were designed so that they were three metres further apart at the centre than at the ends. This arrangement is found in other ancient stadia and was copied in the modern Olympic stadium in Athens (see p.14).

22 Judges' stand

A platform at the southern edge of the course, just under one third of the way from the western end, supported seats for the judges. Almost certainly those who were

(*Below*) The judges' stand in the stadium. The space in front of the seats may have been used for the prizegiving ceremony, when perhaps the gold and ivory table for the wreaths was brought from the Temple of Hera. Apart from the foundations, no trace of the seats survives, and they have been restored on the basis of illustrations on vases.

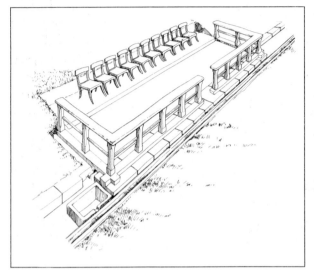

(*Above*) Looking eastward through the tunnel leading into the stadium.

adjudicating a particular event would have stood at the finishing line and the seats were essentially honorary.

23 Entrance tunnel to stadium

The embankment at the west end of the stadium at Olympia required the construction of an entrance tunnel leading into the stadium from the Altis. This tunnel, which was thirty-two metres long with a vaulted roof, was the earliest example of such a structure in classical Greece. It was reserved for the use of judges and contestants only, and the western end of the tunnel could be closed by bronze trellis gates. The emergence into the stadium of the grand procession was a highlight of the festival. The tunnel was so well hidden beneath the earth embankment that Pausanias calls it the 'Secret Entrance'. Here the eager, anxious athletes must have waited to be summoned into the stadium for their particular contest. The tunnel into the stadium at Nemea is better preserved and tantalising fragments of graffiti by known Olympic victors have survived, conveying a very human aspect of the games.

24 Gymnasium

This magnificent building was constructed during the second century BC. It is adjacent to the palaistra and both structures were probably for the use of competitors only. The great length of the gymnasium was determined by the fact that the eastern colonnade housed a double running track, 197.28 metres long, exactly the distance of the track in the stadium. This we know because sills similar to those in the stadium were found in place at each end of the colonnade. The athletes could practise here during bad weather on a floor of levelled earth. The courtyard of

The palaistra and
gymnasium from the
south.

the gymnasium was large enough to accommodate additional running tracks and
space for discus- and javelin-throwing.

Around the middle of the second century BC the Eleans made an impressive
addition to the gymnasium in the form of a majestic, triple-arched gateway at the
south-east corner. It must have been an imposing sight for those approaching the
gymnasium from the northern entrance of the Altis.

No trace of the western half of the building remains today. In antiquity the river
Kladeos was kept to its course west of the Altis by a retaining wall (Plan 34), but
when it burst its banks and flooded the sanctuary, in the fourth century AD,
approximately half the gymnasium was swept away, including what Pausanias calls
the living quarters for the athletes. The Kladeos never returned to its original course
and today it forms the western limit of the excavated part of the sanctuary. The
eastern end of the northern colonnade was detected during trial excavations before
the Second World War, but the modern road and present usage of the area north of
it have prevented any further investigations.

25 Palaistra

Training in combat and jumping events took place in the *palaistra*. There was
usually at least one palaistra in every city from the sixth century BC until the end of
the Roman Empire. They were often privately owned, and people using the
facilities were required to be members. It was not only a place for exercise but also a
kind of social club, and just as it is customary now for friends to meet for a round of
golf or a game of squash, then they would have enjoyed a bout of wrestling or
boxing, followed by idle gossip or perhaps an intellectual discussion. According to
Plato, Socrates and Alkibiades were often to be found engaged in these activities.

A view from one of the rooms in the north-eastern corner of the palaistra, looking south westward through the double colonnade across the inner courtyard.
The columns were re-erected recently to give the visitor an idea of the general layout of the building.
In the foreground is a statue-base, and behind it runs one of the drains that form an intricate network across the site.

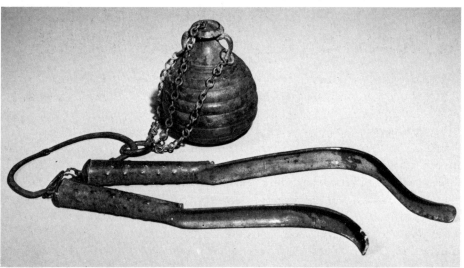

Before exercise athletes would rub olive oil on to their skin.
The oil was kept in a small flask called an *aryballos (left)* which was often tied on to the wrist.
The oil helped to prevent sunburn, and stopped dirt from getting into the pores.
Afterwards a strigil was used to scrape off the oil and dirt *(opposite, right)*.
Aryballos (height 6.8 cm) and two strigils on a chain.
Roman. BMC Bronzes 2455.

The palaistra at Olympia, which was built in the third century BC, followed the standard design for this type of building. It was a courtyard surrounded by four colonnades, at the backs of which were a number of rooms. Vitruvius, the Roman architect, wrote down the specifications for a palaistra, and with the aid of his information and the evidence of the excavations, it is possible to identify the use of most of the nineteen chambers. An oiling-room, called an *eliothesium*, and a powdering room, called a *konisterium*, (see p.57) opened off from the *ephebeium*, a common room for athletes in the centre of the north wing. This was the only room to have a marble floor; the rest had tamped down soil or clay. The *ephebeium* also had access to the *gymnasium*.

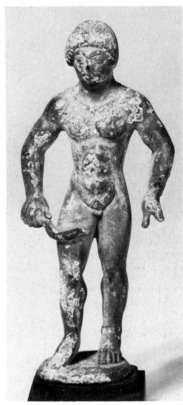

(Above) One athlete helps another to rinse off the dust and sand from his hair. From a Greek drinking-cup, 475–450 BC. BMC Vases E 83.

(Above, right) Etruscan bronze statuette, *c.* 500 BC, height 10.7 cm. BM Reg. no. 1907. 10–20. 1

At the eastern end of the north colonnade was a spacious cold bath and, at the western end, a washroom. The bathing arrangements in a palaistra were usually more elaborate but at Olympia the athletes were already well provided with separate facilities for this purpose (see p.29).

One of the main functions of the palaistra was to offer indoor facilities for the athletes during bad weather. All of the rooms except two, one in the west and one in the east wing, had benches all round for spectators. The exceptions are likely to be the *coryceum*, an exercise room which housed a punchbag, and an indoor training area for wrestlers. The long room in the southern colonnade would have been ideal for jumping practice. Any indoor or outdoor activity could be watched from the colonnades.

The purpose of a tiled area in the northern part of the courtyard at Olympia remains a mystery. It is composed of fluted tiles save for a narrow strip of plain tiles running lengthwise down the centre. It has been suggested that this area may have been used as some type of bowling alley. On the face of it this seems unlikely; however, the discovery of a similar arrangement in the Baths at Pompeii, with two large stone balls still in place on the tiles, makes a game of this sort a real possibility.

26 Bathing facilities and water supply

Baths existed at Olympia as early as the fifth century BC. Their existence at this stage is a measure of the importance which the Greeks attached to bathing after exercise.

Until this time washing facilities for athletes at Olympia had been fairly primitive and they made do with cold water in the wash room of the palaistra or gymnasium. Before these buildings were constructed, the athletes had used water from wells and basins, but by the fifth century, despite opposition, better facilities were coming into vogue. Many people condemned the arrival of hot baths as a sign of weakness: Plato thought them fit only for the old and feeble, while Aristophanes complained that the athletes were deserting the palaistra and going to the baths instead.

The early installations in the west of the Altis contained hip-baths and a hearth where water could be heated. The building which later became the Heroon, or shrine of an unnamed hero, was also originally a bath-house, containing the earliest known Greek vapour-bath. Water was heated in huge bronze cauldrons in the southern room, and steam was then created by plunging them into cold water in the circular pool. The room to the west of this was the *apodyterion*, or changing room. By 100 BC, however, the vapour-bath had fallen into disuse. The baths in the west had been demolished and in their place appeared something quite new in Greece at that time – a Roman-type bath with underfloor heating known as a hypocaust, providing both hot water and steam baths.

The intricate system of drains and channels which honeycomb the site at Olympia is indeed as remarkable as the buildings themselves. Good drainage was essential since the area tended to be marshlike in the wetter seasons. However, the availability of fresh water was always a problem, particularly since the Kladeos tended to recede considerably and stagnate during the summer. A small supply came from springs to the north, but the problem was not substantially alleviated until the second century AD, when the Roman millionaire, Herodes Atticus, constructed a magnificent fountain complex at the western end of the Treasuries.

27 Swimming Pool

This modern-looking open-air pool was unique in classical Greece. Built in the fifth century BC it was 24 metres long by 16 metres wide and 1.60 metres deep, with steps leading down into it from each side.

28 Hippodrome

The *hippodrome* (literally 'horse-track') at Olympia will remain the most enigmatic area of the site. Pausanias tells us that it was to the east of the Altis and south of the stadium, but by the Middle Ages the river Alpheios had flooded its banks and completely washed away every feature in that area. To increase the difficulty of reconstruction, no other Greek hippodrome has left any informative remains. This is to be expected, as there was usually no special building associated with a hippodrome. An open stretch of level ground, often used at other times as grazing land, was all that was required. By preference it would be in a valley or at least at the foot of a hill to afford the spectators a good viewpoint. The only seating was for the judges and perhaps a few privileged guests, while the rest of the spectators jostled with one another for the best vantage points. Artificial banks were often added later. A source of water in the immediate vicinity was essential to satisfy the thirst of both men and horses.

In the absence of any other evidence for the actual appearance of the hippodrome at Olympia, we must rely on surviving literary evidence; this entails gathering scattered references which range from a somewhat unsatisfactory description by Pausanias, to measurements included in an eleventh-century manuscript found in the old Seraglio at Istanbul. The hippodrome was clearly on a larger and more elaborate scale than was customary. It is possible to estimate that the total length of the track was six hundred metres (slightly over one-third of a mile) and that its width was in the region of two hundred metres. An average lap therefore would cover over twelve hundred metres (just under three-quarters of a mile).

Pausanias says that the hippodrome was flanked by rising ground in the north and by an earth embankment in the south. For many years before the flooding this artificial bank served the dual purpose of accommodating the spectators and providing a barrier against the winter torrents of the Alpheios. We also know the approximate position of the judges' seats – to the western end of the northern bank, since Pausanias recalls arriving at them after clambering over the south bank of the stadium. This chance comment shows the fortuitous nature of our sources of knowledge for the hippodrome.

Two pillars were erected on the course to mark the turns; the one in the west also served to indicate the start and finish. In some of the scenes on pottery depicting horse-races this marker appears to be a portable wooden column, which we occasionally see knocked over. However at Olympia it was a permanent structure, surmounted by bronze statues representing Hippodomeia crowning Pelops (see p.66). Surviving representations of Greek horse-events do not show the barrier which extended between the posts of the later Roman race course.

No doubt some kind of barrier ran round the perimeter of the track to protect the crowd from bolting horses or chariots careering out of control. There would have been gates in the barrier, for the removal of wreckage and injured parties.

29 Starting gate for horse-races

The most remarkable feature of the hippodrome at Olympia was the starting apparatus, called the *aphesis*. This elaborate mechanism was much admired in antiquity. It was designed by Cleoetas, son of Aristokles, about whom unfortunately we know nothing, other than that he was proud enough to boast on the

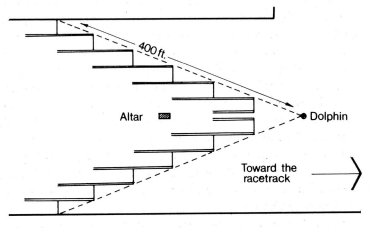

A schematic reconstruction of the *aphesis*, or starting apparatus, in the hippodrome; in reality there were probably at least twenty traps for horses and chariots. According to Pausanias there were many more altars in the vicinity, which we cannot now locate with accuracy.

400 ft.

Altar

Dolphin

Toward the racetrack

base of his statue in Athens that he invented 'the way of starting for the horses at Olympia'. The only surviving description of the apparatus is to be found in Pausanias' *Description of Greece*, VI 20.10–13:

'*The starting place is shaped like the prow of a ship, the beak being turned towards the course. . . At the very tip of the beak is a bronze dolphin on a rod. Each side of the starting place is more than four hundred feet long, and in each of the sides, stalls are built. These are assigned to the competitors by lot. In front of the chariots or race-horses stretches a rope as a barrier. An altar of unburnt brick, plastered over on the outside, is made every Olympiad as nearly as possible to the middle of the prow. On the altar is a bronze eagle, with its wings spread to the full. The starter sets the machinery in the altar going, whereupon up jumps the eagle into the view of the spectators, and down falls the dolphin to the ground. The first ropes to be let go are those at the furthest ends of the prow, and the horses stationed here are the first off. Away they go until they come neck and neck with the chariots that have drawn the second stations. Then the ropes at the second stations are released. And so it runs on till all the chariots are abreast of each other at the beak of the prow. After that it is for the charioteers to display their skill and the horses their speed.*'

The general principles of the aphesis are clear, but there are insufficient details to make a definite reconstruction. We do not know how many competitors took part; Pindar speaks of a race in the hippodrome at Delphi where forty entrants competed, out of which Arkesilas was the sole finisher, but this was probably an exceptionally large field. The aphesis at Olympia was apparently not designed for any practical purpose: it made no attempt at a staggered start. Clearly the object of such a feat of engineering was spectacle; it provided the sight of pent-up horses and colourful chariots successively bursting forth from their traps, and battling for the lead right from the very start.

3 The Games

Our sources of knowledge for the Games

We have no manual of Greek athletics; it is evident that in antiquity trainers could refer to textbooks containing exercises for physical prowess, but unfortunately only a few fragmentary passages on scraps of papyrus have survived.

Luckily other sources do exist, and many will be referred to in the following pages. Most informative are the scenes represented on contemporary pottery as the Greeks decorated a great many of their vessels with aspects of daily life. Another source of information is the coinage of certain city-states, depicting an athletic event with which they were particularly associated. Furthermore a number of statues of athletes still exist, although most are Roman copies of Greek originals. It was customary for statues to record the achievements of successful athletes at the Games; many were of bronze, as this was believed to be the most durable of materials, but sadly in later years the value of the metal caused the statues to be melted down for other uses. Marble survives better than bronze although it can be broken up for building material or burnt to provide lime for mortar. Through the course of the centuries thousands of statues were plundered from Greek sanctuaries, many to be included in the collections of Roman aristocrats, but the vast majority were ultimately destroyed. Often only the statue-bases have survived, and from the inscriptions on them it is possible to glean a few details about the athlete who was commemorated and the event he won. Other official inscriptions provide some of the regulations for the athletic festivals and details about the officials who were in charge of them.

Finally, there are the literary sources. Contemporary Greek literature contains a number of incidental references to the Games, notably the Victory Hymns of Pindar which were composed to honour the athletes of his day. There is also a quantity of written information from the Roman period, which must be studied with caution when it refers to events which took place several hundred years before the time of the writer. Nonetheless these are invaluable documents since it is unlikely that the events changed a great deal over the years due to their religious connotations. The most prolific writer on the Olympic festival and on the site was Pausanias, who wrote a travel-guide to Greece in the second century AD. Another lengthy text survives from a treatise *On Gymnastics* by Philostratos of Lemnos, who wrote during the second and third centuries AD. It contains some interesting details, but sadly the author appears to have had little, if any, practical experience of athletics himself, and the book was probably written as an intellectual exercise. Very little survives of the official lists of victors. Part of the list of winners in the foot-race survives, as an extract was incorporated into a Roman work of the fourth century AD, and by chance the names of some of the victors from the fifth century BC have been preserved on the back of a Roman financial account.

These are the pieces of information which must be fitted together like a jigsaw

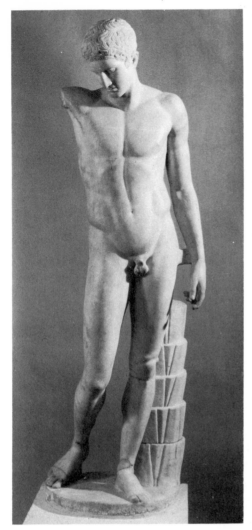

(*Left*) The 'Westmacott Athlete', a Roman marble copy of a Greek work of about 440 BC. The original was perhaps the statue of the boxer Kyniskos by Polykleitos, which Pausanias saw at Olympia; the inscribed base for this was found during the excavations, and the cuttings for the feet correspond well with the stance of this figure. The popularity of Greek works of art among the Romans, following the plundering of many cities and sanctuaries in Greece, led to the production of numerous copies. Height 1.5 m. BMC Sculpture 1754.

(*Below*) A seated official who may well be a judge, or *hellanodikas*, since a starting or finishing post stands behind him. From a Greek storage-jar, 475–450 BC. BMC Vases E 342.

An instructor (*right*) supervises a training session. The discus-thrower is poised at the farthest point of his backward swing, while the athlete on the ground binds a thong around a javelin. Beside him are a pick used for breaking up the pitch, and a pair of jumping weights. Rhythm is provided by a pipe-player whose cheeks are bound to prevent any disfiguration of the face. From the shoulder of a water-jar, *c.* 510–500 BC. BMC Vases E 164.

puzzle, to provide a picture which, although incomplete, is sufficient to show what the Games were like in antiquity.

Preparation and training

'If you have worked hard enough to render yourself worthy of going to Olympia, if you have not been idle or ill-disciplined, then go with confidence; but those who have not trained in this fashion, let them go where they will.'

Philostratus the Elder, second century AD, *Apollonius of Tyana* v 43

The Olympic Festival lasted for five days but the preparations took virtually the whole of the preceding year. Strangely, there is no firm evidence that the sports facilities at Olympia were used during the period between the festivals. Local villagers may have exercised there but they would have been few in number. Much hard physical labour was therefore required to get things ready. Any undergrowth that had sprung up had to be cleared. The courses had to be dug and levelled and the sand pits prepared. Repairs and general tidying up of the buildings and monuments in and around the sanctuary were also necessary.

Ten months to go

The most important officials at the Games, who were known as the *Hellanodikai*, commenced preparations ten months before the games were due to start. Their name means literally 'judges of the Greeks', reflecting the national character of the Games. In the early years of the festival they had been referred to merely as *agonothetai*, 'games organisers'. They had their own special residence in Elis called the *hellanodikaion*. The Hellanodikai were chosen by lot, and although their numbers fluctuated, there were ten for most of the history of the Games. One of them acted as the overall supervisor while the rest were divided into three groups, each presiding over different events. The first group organised the equestrian events, the second the pentathlon, and the third the remainder of the competitions. Throughout the ages the Olympic judges were renowned for their impartiality. They wore robes of purple, the royal colour serving as a reminder of the time when King Iphitos controlled the Games and officiated as the sole judge. The athletes, too, had to be in strict training in their home towns during the ten months prior to the Games and they had to swear to this effect.

One month to go

For at least one month before the festival prospective competitors in the Games were required to reside at Elis and train under the strict supervision of the Hellanodikai. There were three gymnasiums at Elis and in addition the local market place was stripped and used as a practice track for the horse races. This period of compulsory training at Elis was enforced by the Eleans probably to demonstrate their absolute control over the Games. Their authority had been contested in the past particularly by their neighbours the Pisatans, but eventually the Eleans established supremacy. During this month the judges were fully occupied with various tasks: they disqualified those who were not fit, checked on parentage and Greek descent, and resolved any disputes concerning the classification of men and boys, horses and colts. The training was renowned for its harshness: the athletes had to observe a strict diet, carry out a gruelling regime of exercise and obey every word of the Hellanodikai. It is not certain when the period of compulsory training was introduced, but since it required the athlete to be away from home for a considerable time he had to be fairly affluent. Sometimes his father or brother would accompany him to Elis but more often a private trainer had to be employed. By this time the era of the amateur athlete was clearly coming to a close.

Two days to go

Two days before the festival began the whole company set out from Elis, which was roughly fifty-eight kilometres from Olympia. First came the Hellanodikai and other officials, then the athletes and their trainers, horses and chariots together with their owners, jockeys and charioteers. They followed the Sacred Way along the coast, stopping to sacrifice a pig and to perform other rites at the fountain of Piera on the boundary between Elis and Olympia. They spent the night at Letrini and the next day wound their way along the valley of the Alpheios towards the Altis.

The scene is set

Meanwhile people from all walks of life had been making their way to Olympia. Princes and tyrants from Sicily and southern Italy sailed up the river in splendid barges; ambassadors came from various towns, vying with each other in dress and paraphernalia. The rich came on horseback, and in chariots; the poor came on donkeys, in carts and even on foot. Food-sellers came loaded with supplies for there was no town near Olympia. Merchants flocked in with their wares. Artisans came to make figurines that pilgrims could buy to offer to their god. Booths and stalls were set up; tents and huts were erected, for only official delegates were given accommodation in the magnificent guest-house known as the *Leonidaion*. Most visitors looked for a suitable spot to put down their belongings and slept each night under the summer skies.

The crowds were so great that by sunrise on the first day of the Games there was not a single space left from which to see the events.

Two days before the Olympic festival, the judges, trainers and competitors set out from Elis along the Sacred Way to Olympia, a distance of about fifty-eight kilometres.

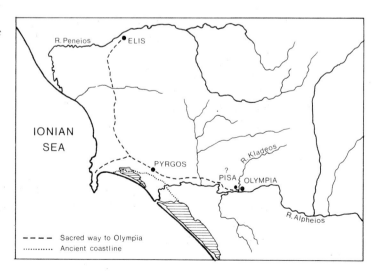

36

4 The Programme

Day One   **Morning** Swearing-in ceremony for competitors and judges in the Bouleuterion (Council-House) before the altar and statue of Zeus *Horkios* (Zeus of the Oaths).
Contests for heralds and trumpeters held near the stadium entrance.
Boys' running, wrestling and boxing contests.
Public and private prayers and sacrifices in the Altis; consultation of oracles.

Afternoon Orations by well-known philosophers and recitals by poets and historians.
Sightseeing tours of the Altis.
Reunions with old friends.

Day Two   **Morning** Procession into the hippodrome of all those competing there.
Chariot- and horse-races.

Afternoon The pentathlon: discus, javelin, jumping, running and wrestling.

Evening Funeral rites in honour of the hero Pelops.
Parade of victors round the Altis.
Communal singing of victory hymns.
Feasting and revelry.

Day Three   **Morning** Procession of the Hellanodikai (Judges), ambassadors from the Greek states, competitors in all events and sacrificial animals round the Altis to the Great Altar in front of the Temple of Zeus, followed by the official sacrifice of one hundred oxen given by the people of Elis.

Afternoon Foot-races.

Evening Public banquet in the Prytaneion.

Day Four   **Morning** Wrestling.
Midday Boxing and the *pankration*.
Afternoon Race-in-armour.

Day Five   Procession of victors to the Temple of Zeus where they are crowned with wreaths of wild olive by the Hellanodikai, followed by the *phyllobolia* (when the victors are showered with leaves and flowers).
Feasting and celebrations.

This programme is hypothetical since it contains not only all the events held around 100 BC (the period represented by the model), but also, for interest, various contests which had been discontinued by that time. The dates when the various events were introduced are listed below. The order of contests at the festival is based as accurately as possible on the surviving literary evidence.

Dates for the introduction of events

Olympiad	Year, BC	Event
I	776	Stade-race (short foot-race)
14	724	*Diaulos* (double-length foot-race)
15	720	*Dolichos* (long-distance foot-race)
18	708	*Pentathlon* and wrestling
23	688	Boxing
25	680	*Tethrippon* (four-horse chariot-race)
33	648	*Pankration* (type of all-in wrestling) and horse-race
37	632	Foot-race and wrestling for boys
38	628	*Pentathlon* for boys (immediately discontinued)
41	616	Boxing for boys
65	520	Race-in-armour
70	500	*Apene* (mule-cart race)
71	496	*Calpe* or *anabates* (race for mares)
84	444	*Apene* and *calpe* discontinued
93	408	*Synoris* (two-horse chariot-race)
96	396	Competitions for heralds and trumpeters
99	384	Chariot-racing for teams of four colts
128	268	Chariot-racing for teams of two colts
131	256	Races for colts
145	200	*Pankration* for boys

Throughout the Games prayers and sacrifices were offered to Zeus and other gods. This is a thank-offering in honour of a victory. Nike, or Victory personified, flies over the altar while a wreathed man superintends the sacrifice; two athletes are ready to roast pieces of meat on spits over the fire on the altar, on which there is a large hook or horn of an ox. The pipe-player on the right provides music for the ceremony. Greek storage-jar, 475–450 BC. BMC Vases E 455.

Public and Private Sacrifices

The great sacrifice to Zeus of one hundred oxen took place on the morning of the middle day of the festival, that is immediately after the full moon. The Greeks reckoned their day from sunset to sunset, so that the full moon and the sacrifice were both on the same day. After the procession had reached the great altar of Zeus the oxen were slaughtered, and their legs were carried to the top of the mound of ashes which had accumulated from previous sacrifices. There they were burned in honour of the god, who was believed to take sustenance from the smoke. The mortal attendants of the festival, however, took their nourishment from the rest of the ox-flesh which was roasted later for the public banquet.

The grand procession round the Altis gave the various Greek ambassadors the opportunity to show off their wealth and finery, in particular the ceremonial vessels belonging to their city-states which would be used for the banquet. Alkibiades, the Athenian statesman, once embarrassed his city by using the official gold and silver plate for his own private victory celebrations on the night before.

Many minor sacrifices were made throughout the festival. There were numerous altars and statues of deities in the sanctuary, and here the athletes would pray, make vows and offer thanks. Sometimes they would consult the innards of a sacrificed animal to see whether they foretold victory. The priests who resided at Olympia carried out sacrifices at sixty-nine of the altars regularly each month of every year and, furthermore, there was a programme of daily offerings or libations of wine for Zeus alone.

A young boxer, grasping his *himantes* or boxing thongs in one hand, extends the other hand towards an altar in an attitude of prayer.
Interior of a Greek drinking-cup, 500–475 BC.
BMC Vases E 39.

A model of an altar decorated with a *bukranion* (ox-skull) and swathes of foliage; flames twist upward from a pile of logs on top.
Roman, height 7.3 cm.
BMC Bronzes 881.

5 Rules

'But the Zeus in the Bouleuterion is of all the images of Zeus most likely to strike terror into the hearts of sinners. He is surnamed Horkios [*Oath god*] *and in each hand he holds a thunderbolt. Beside this image it is the custom for athletes, their fathers and their brothers, as well as their trainers, to swear an oath upon slices of boar's flesh that in nothing will they sin against the Olympic Games. . .'*
Pausanias, second century AD, *Description of Greece* V 24.9

This was the oath taken by the athletes at the start of each Olympic festival. In addition the Hellanodikai had to swear that they would judge fairly and keep secret anything that they had learned about a competitor.

They were entirely responsible for the enforcement of rules and regulations and acted as both judges and umpires; they also meted out punishment for any infringements. The penalties were harsh: both competitors and trainers who failed to comply with instructions could be publicly whipped by the *mastigophorai* (whip-bearers), a form of punishment usually reserved for slaves. Heavy fines were occasionally imposed, especially in cases of bribery, which was regarded as a particularly odious crime. As a warning to potential offenders money from such fines was used to pay for bronze statues of Zeus (known as *Zanes*, a dialect form of Zeus) which were set up along the terrace wall leading to the entrance of the stadium (Plan 30). According to Pausanias, there were sixteen of these in all, six of which were erected from fines levied on the city of Athens, when Kallipos, an Athenian, bribed his opponents in the pentathlon. Athens refused to pay until the Delphic oracle threatened that there would be no more prophecies unless the fine was paid in full. Instances of bribery were relatively rare, and Pausanias remarked that it was incredible for any man to have so little respect for the god and even more incredible 'that one of the Eleans themselves should fall so low'. This was Damonikos, the parent of a boy athlete who was over-anxious for his son's success. He had bribed the father of his son's opponent, and on discovery both the fathers were fined.

It must often have been difficult to decide the winner, particularly in the foot- and horse-races, where the judges had to rely on eyesight; there was of course no such thing as a photo-finish. There was only one victor; coming second or third counted for nothing. In the event of a draw the crown was dedicated to the god.

Women at Olympia

'On the road to Olympia. . .there is a precipitous mountain with lofty cliffs. . .the mountain is called Typaeum. It is a law of Elis that any woman who is discovered at the Olympic Games will be pitched headlong from this mountain.'
Pausanias, second century AD, *Description of Greece* V 6.7

Apparently this ban applied only to married women as Pausanias states elsewhere that 'virgins were not refused admission'. No written evidence survives to explain this discrimination, but it is possible that the practice dated back to the fertility games of the remote past when only virgins were considered pure enough to attend the sacred rites. If this was the original reason then it had been long forgotten, for Dio Chrysostom says that 'even women of dubious character' were allowed at the panhellenic games.

There was one married woman who was actually required to witness the Games; she was the priestess of Demeter Chamyne. The marble altar of the goddess (Plan 31) was situated halfway along the north bank of the stadium, and on this the priestess sat to observe the Games. Demeter was the goddess linked with vegetation and fertility and the epithet *Chamyne*, meaning 'of the couch', may again refer back to some fertility ritual. This would have been before the Games were established in honour of Zeus.

Only one other married woman is known to have gained admittance to the Games. She was called either Kallipateira or Pherenike, and she was the daughter of Diagoras, the famous boxer from Rhodes (p.65). As her husband was dead, she disguised herself as a trainer and brought her son Pisirodos to Olympia to compete. Pisirodos won, and in her excitement the mother leapt over the barrier of the trainers' enclosure and in so doing exposed herself. But the authorities let her go unpunished out of respect for her father, brothers and son, all of whom had won Olympic victories. As a precaution, however, they passed a law that in future the trainers, like the athletes, must be naked when they came to be registered.

Women themselves were definitely not allowed to compete in the Olympics. But this did not prevent them from participating indirectly. As owners of horses there was no law to prevent them from entering their teams in the chariot events, and several women are known to have done this at Olympia. The first and most famous of all was Kyniska, daughter of King Archidamos of Sparta. Plutarch, the Greek biographer who lived in the first and second centuries AD, says that her brother Agesilaos persuaded her to enter a chariot in one of the races, in order to prove that victory in equestrian events was a result of wealth and nothing to do with skill.

But, according to Pausanias, Kyniska had always had one great ambition – to win an Olympic victory. This she achieved, and in celebration of the event she set up two bronze monuments representing chariots, a small one in the antechamber of the temple of Zeus, and a larger one in the grounds of the Altis. Part of the inscribed base of the larger monument has been found and indicates that it included a statue of herself. An ancient source recorded the full wording of the inscription:

Sparta's kings were fathers and brothers of mine,
But since with my chariot and storming horses I, Kyniska,
Have won the prize, I place my effigy here
And proudly proclaim
That of all Grecian women I first bore the crown.
Greek Anthology XIII 16, after Drees

The Games of Hera

Women were excluded from competing in the Olympic Games, but they did have a festival of their own at Olympia. This was the *Heraia*, or games held in honour of Hera. These were also celebrated every four years, but there was only one type of event – the foot-race. It was divided into three separate contests for girls of different age-groups. Pausanias provides details about the organisation of these games, which were the responsibility of sixteen of the most respected women of Elis, each aided by an assistant. This tradition was traced back to the wedding celebrations of Hippodameia, who chose sixteen matrons to help her inaugurate the Heraia (see p.66).

The track in the stadium was shortened by one sixth especially for the contests, making it just over one hundred and sixty metres. The winners were given crowns of olive like the Olympic victors, and they also received a portion of a heifer sacrificed to Hera. Just as the Olympic prize-winners were allowed to dedicate statues of themselves, so the girl victors were granted the privilege of setting up their images in the temple of Hera. Evidence suggests that these were paintings rather than statues.

Religious conservatism is probably the reason why no other competitions were ever introduced for women at Olympia, even though by the Christian era most of the major Greek games incorporated women's events. At Sparta girls seem always to have undertaken the same athletic exercises as boys, as tough, strong mothers were believed to produce good Spartan soldiers. Even Plato, composing the guidelines for his ideal state, advocated running and fencing for women, but he stressed that after the age of thirteen they should wear 'appropriate dress'.

This bronze statuette of a girl runner probably comes from Sparta, where women were expected to take part in athletics. Her appearance corresponds well with Pausanias' description of the girls who raced in the Heraia:
'their hair hangs down, a tunic reaches to a little above the knee, and they bare the right shoulder as far as the breast'.
Description of Greece v 16.4.
c. 500 BC.
Height 11.4 cm.
BMC Bronzes 208.

6 Events

Athletics

'Charmos, a long-distance runner, finished seventh in a field of six. A friend ran alongside him shouting, "Keep going, Charmos!" and although fully dressed, beat him. And if he had had five friends he would have finished twelfth.'
Nikarchos, first century AD, *Palatine Anthology*, XI 82, after Harris.

Running

It was the *stade*- or short foot-race that determined the length of the stadium at Olympia. This was the most ancient and indeed the only event at the first thirteen Olympiads. The winner of the stade-race had the Olympiad named after him and the esteem in which he was held is indicated by the custom of dating by reference to the list of victors. Gradually other foot-races were added to the programme at Olympia. The *diaulos*, named after the musical double-pipes, consisted of two lengths of the stadium while the *dolichos* was a long-distance race, consisting of twenty or twenty-four lengths. It was used as an opening event, no doubt because it was the longest and least spectacular race, and gave the spectators a chance to settle down. The dolichos, the diaulos and the stade-race seem to have been features of all the major athletic festivals. The exceptional athlete who, like Polites in AD 69, won all three events at the same Olympiad, was called a *triastes* or 'tripler'. The greatest Olympic runner of all was Leonidas of Rhodes, who, 'with the speed of a god', won all three events at each of the four successive Olympiads between 164 and 152 BC. For a runner to maintain such a peak of fitness (all the running events were held on the same day) for twelve years, was a remarkable feat, and such was the pride of his countrymen that he became worshipped as a local deity.

There also existed at Olympia the *hoplitodromos* or race-in-armour. This was the last of the foot-races to be added to the programme, in 520 BC. Competitors wore a helmet and greaves and carried a round shield, although it is possible that in later years both helmet and greaves were discarded. Twenty-five runners were allowed to take part, for whom a set of shields was kept in the Temple of Zeus. Presumably this was to ensure that each athlete carried a shield of the same weight. In some of the games contestants were decked out in armour from head to foot. A curious, clanking race, it must have had both serious and comic connotations: serious because all athletic training was devised to keep the male citizen population physically fit for war. Its position at the very end of the festival left a final reminder of this to the assembled crowds. However amusing mishaps and collisions inevitably occurred. On scenes from pottery we often see athletes who have dropped their shields and are stooping to pick them up. The Greeks themselves must have considered it something of a diversion, since when Peisthetairos, a character in Aristophanes' *Birds*, sees the Chorus advancing in their feathered costumes, he likens the motley crew to the armed runners in the hoplitodromos.

At other games there were various additions to the programme. One was the *hippios* or 'horsey' race, probably referring to the fact that it was the same distance as the horse-race, i.e. six stades, or three circuits of the stadium. A curtain raiser at some festivals was the *lampadedromia*, a relay race with a torch as a baton, contested by teams of six to ten in which the winner was the first to arrive home with his torch still alight. As a reward he was granted the honour of lighting the fire on the

A judge watches two armed runners coming past the finishing post.
The winner has taken off his helmet and looks round at the other competitor who has flung down his shield.
The shield device appears to be some kind of plant.
A drinking-cup made in Athens 500–475 BC.
Height 9.2 cm.
Diameter 22.5 cm.
BMC Vases E 818.

(*Left*) Armed runners taking part in the *hoplitodromos* or race-in-armour.
This scene is from a panathenaic amphora, a prize-vessel which was one of a number presented, full of olive oil, to a victor in the panathenaic festival at Athens.
These jars, decorated with the event for which they were awarded, are a useful source for illustrations of athletics.
This vessel can be dated exactly to the year 336 BC as the reigning *archon*, or chief magistrate, is named on the other side.
BMC Vases B 608.

(*Above*) A runner, poised to take off in the customary upright starting position. This miniature *lekythos*, or oil-jar, height 11 cm, and made in Athens about 450–425 BC, was either a toy or an offering. Perspective on Greek vases is a matter of convention rather than accuracy, for in reality the runner stood beside the post with his toes gripping the grooves in the sill.

(*Above, right*) Bronze statuette of a trumpeter from Southern Italy. Competitions for trumpeters and heralds were held on the first day of the festival. The winners signalled the start and announced the results of the other competitions. *c.* 470 BC. Height 14.6 cm. BMC Bronzes 223.

(*Right*) A starting sill in the stadium at Olympia, with grooves for the runner's toes. In the foreground is one of the basins that provided water for the spectators.

The steady rhythm of three long-distance runners forms a strong contrast with the vigorous action of a sprinter.

(Right) Panathenaic amphora made in 333 BC.
BMC Vases B 609.

(Below) Amphora made in eastern Greece
c. 550–525 BC.
BM reg. no. 1864.10–7.156.

sacrificial altar. Despite the fact that the modern Olympics have borrowed the concept of this event as a symbol for the Games, it was definitely not part of the ancient Olympic festival.

There is one foot-race that has not been mentioned so far and that is the 'marathon', which is an entirely modern event. It is true that, according to Greek tradition, some ancient runners were able to cover amazing distances. The most famous is the original 'marathon runner' Pheidippides, who covered 260 kilometres of rugged terrain in less than two days. When in 490 BC the Athenians learned that the Persians had landed at Marathon *en route* to attack Athens, he ran to Sparta with a request for help. Another remarkable achievement occurred in the fourth century BC when Drymos ran all the way from Elis to Epidauros to announce his own Olympic victory, – a journey via the mountains of Arcadia of over 130 kilometres. But the concept of any cross-country event at an athletic festival was totally alien to ancient Greek sport.

'They're off!'

Like modern athletes, before taking their places at the starting line, the runners did a few warming-up exercises, which the Roman poet Statius describes as running on the spot, dropping on to the haunches, beating the chest, sprinting forward and coming to an abrupt halt. Then they stood panting and impatient, ready for the crucial test. Often a great many contestants would enter for the races, and so earlier in the day the runners would draw lots from a bronze bowl or helmet to settle the heats, so that only the very best would be pitted against one another in the final.

The starting position was quite different from that used today. An ancient athlete did not crouch down like his modern counterpart; instead he used a standing start with arms stretched forward, one foot slightly in front of the other, left or right according to preference, and toes firmly gripping the grooves in the marble sill (see p.46).

The signal for the off was given either by the herald's trumpet or by the shout *Apite* – 'Go!'. Those who jumped the start suffered the severe punishment of being flogged by the policeman known as the *alytes*. The greatest burst of speed would always be in the first stretch in order to get clear of the post, and this part of the course, as in the hippodrome, must have been the likeliest place for collisions, fouls and cheating, including taking a short cut without rounding the post, which was only too tempting amid a throng of runners.

In some of the surviving scenes the post seems to have been fitted with a large base to minimise the risk of the runners grabbing hold of it to swing themselves round, which would be a natural impulse. Other familiar faults were holding, tripping or running in front of an opponent.

Just as today, styles of running varied according to the race. The postures of figures on the vases are not always entirely accurate since artists relied heavily on conventional poses, but nevertheless they are an informative guide. Sprinters display the most vigour, arms and legs darting furiously to and fro in a flat-out dash down the track. The dolichos-runner, on the other hand, reserved his energy by keeping his arms bent up close to his sides, and swinging them in relatively relaxed fashion. Only on the final lap did he suddenly spurt toward the finishing post making violent arm movements like the sprinter. Presumably the technique of the diaulos runner was somewhere midway between the two. In remarking on the physical requirements of the two types of runner, Philostratos recommends that the long-distance man should have slender legs and strength in the neck and shoulders, since he needed to swing his arms for a much greater distance.

Nearly all the scenes depicted on pottery show athletes competing nude. Both Homer and Thucydides, however, record that in earlier times athletes wore a type of shorts. Two reasons were given for their discontinuation: one is that a runner competing at Athens was in the lead when unfortunately his shorts came adrift, and he tripped and fell over them. The archon Hippomenes then passed a law that, to avoid future accidents of this nature, all athletes were to perform naked. According to the second version, Orrhippos or Orsippos of Megara won the stade-race at Olympia in 720 BC, but lost his shorts in the process and thus set a new trend. A more likely reason is that Greek men were always proud of their muscular, sun-tanned bodies, and were only too eager to contrast their excellent physical condition with that of barbarians who preferred to keep themselves covered up. We know that runners, like other sportsmen, liberally oiled their skin before an event. The poet Bacchylides tells how Aglaos of Athens rushed into the cheering crowds at the end of a race and bespattered the spectators' garments with oil.

At the end of each contest the names of the victor, his father and his city-state were proclaimed by the herald. Most important of all was the winner of the stade-race, for, as he had won the most hallowed of all races, the Olympiad was named after him.

The pentathlon

The *pentathlon* was a test for the all-round athlete. The five events were discus, jumping, javelin, running and wrestling, held in that order during the course of one afternoon. The last two events existed as competitions in their own right but the other three were not found outside the pentathlon. It is not clear just how the winner of the pentathlon was decided, but it seems likely that if an athlete won the first three events, he would be declared the overall winner and the running and wrestling competitions would be cancelled.

In some ways the pentathlete was considered inferior to the athlete who excelled in a particular event, but his skill lay in versatility, and the contest was probably invented to discover the athlete who possessed this quality. The pentathlete's physical appearance was much admired, for the variety of exertion gave him a particularly supple body, which lacked what the Greeks considered to be unsightly, overdeveloped muscles. Aristotle praises their fleetness of foot and strength of build.

For all its moderation the pentathlon was certainly not an undemanding contest. In particular it required great powers of endurance. This is confirmed by the fact that when the boys' pentathlon was introduced at Olympia in 628 BC, it was immediately discontinued, presumably because it was too exacting, and not, as Pausanias would have us believe, because a Spartan won it.

Each of the events of the pentathlon is dealt with under the appropriate heading.

Discus-throwing

'Phlegyas of Pisa. . .first roughens the discus and his own hand with earth; then shaking off the dust he turns it dexterously to see which side best suits his fingers, or fits more snugly the middle of his arm. He had always loved this sport, and used to practise throwing the discus across the Alpheios where the banks are furthest apart, always clearing the river and never getting the discus wet. . .'

Statius, first century AD *Thebaid* VI 670-77

Discus-throwing is a curious sport. Today hardly anyone would question the choice of a circular, flat object as a throwing weight because we appreciate the aerodynamic qualities of this shape. The Greeks, although not aware of the technicalities, realised that the thin, round, water-smoothed pebbles that they found in river-beds could be thrown further and faster than simple stones. Despite this knowledge, stone-throwing, *lithobolos*, existed in several places as a contest in its own right. Normally the stones would have weighed no more than a few kilograms, but the record stone-throw of all time must surely be that of a man called Bubon, for in the museum at Olympia there is a boulder which bears this inscription:

Bubon. . .the son of Pholos, threw me over his head with one hand.

It weighs 143.5 kilograms, nearly 316 lbs.

Although stone-throwing bears some similarities to modern shot-putting it was not included in the ancient Olympic Games, whereas discus-throwing was. Apart from its aerodynamic shape, there was an additional reason for the adoption of the discus. In the *Iliad*, Homer describes the funeral games held in honour of Patroklos before the walls of Troy. Achilles offered a valuable ingot of iron, which was then a precious metal, to the man who could throw it farthest. We know from surviving examples that such ingots were similar in shape to the discus; this was because the metal was poured into open, circular moulds scooped out in the sand, forming ingots curved on one side and flat on the other. The suitability of the object as a throwing weight must have been obvious. Although ingots may have been used in competitions for some years they were eventually replaced by the purpose-made discus. The discus itself was no longer the prize in the competition: it was merely a piece of equipment.

About twenty ancient discuses have survived; most are bronze, a few are marble, and one is lead. They vary in diameter from about 17 to 35 centimetres, with an average thickness of $1\frac{1}{2}$ centimetres. The weights range from approximately $1\frac{1}{2}$ to $6\frac{1}{2}$ kilograms, $2\frac{1}{2}$ kilograms being the average, just half a kilogram more than the minimum weight for a modern discus, which is usually made of wood, with an inner metal plate and rim.

The discrepancies in the weights and measurements of the ancient discuses are not so surprising when we consider that they were not all necessarily intended for actual use; some may have been made expressly as religious offerings. Varying local standards of weight must also be taken into account, plus the fact that discuses of different weights were used for the men's and boys' events. This distinction is implied by Pausanias, who records that some colossal bones, thought to be those of Ajax, were found on Salamis, the knee-cap being 'as big as a boy's discus'.

A discus-thrower depicted on a silver coin from the Greek island of Cos. Beside him is a tripod, a bowl on a three-legged stand, which was given as a prize at some festivals.
Fifth century BC.
Diameter 2.5 cm.
BMC Coins, Cos 8.

A discus-thrower
depicted on a cast
from a Greek
carnelian sealstone.
A strigil hangs
behind him.
Sixth century BC.
17 × 12 mm.
BMC Engraved
Gems & Cameos
481.

At Olympia, three 'official' discuses were kept in the Treasury of the Sikyonians; these would have been used in competitions to ensure fairness. An amusing legend suggests that the Olympic discus was particularly heavy. According to the legend, the ghost of Protesilaos, the first Greek to be killed in the Trojan War, was fifteen feet tall, and haunted a vineyard near Gallipoli; being a kindly soul, he would help the local farmer, but in his spare time, this awesome spectre practised athletics, throwing a discus 'twice the weight of the one being used at Olympia'.

There has been a great deal of discussion about the method of discus-throwing in antiquity. Paintings and sculptures usually depict the discus-thrower in one of several conventional poses, so that it is difficult to reconstruct the whole series of movements. No doubt athletes had their own individual styles just as they do now, but the series of drawings (p.52) illustrates what seems to be the commonest method. There is no evidence that the athlete made more than a three-quarter turn before throwing the discus, whereas today the thrower will spin round two and a half times to give impulsion.

Very little is known about the length of the throws achieved in antiquity, and those which are recorded are something of a surprise. One was made by Phaullos in

(*Above*) A bronze discus thrown by Exoidas when he won a contest in Kephallenia; he dedicated the discus to Castor and Pollux, the twin sons of Zeus. Castor was renowned as a discus-thrower. The spiral inscription is written retrograde (right to left) in archaic Greek lettering. Sixth century BC. Diameter 16.5 cm. Weight 1.25 kilograms. BMC Bronzes 3207.

(*Right*) Marble statue of a discus-thrower: Roman copy of a Greek bronze original, perhaps the famous discus-thrower by the sculptor Myron. First century AD. Height 1.69 m. Townley Collection BMC Sculpture 250.

(*Above*) An attempt to reconstruct the ancient method of discus-throwing.

about 480 BC. He was a somewhat legendary figure who fought in the battle of Salamis and was also a renowned athlete. He won two victories in the pentathlon and one in the foot-race at Delphi, where a statue was erected to record his achievements. Phaullos made the only discus-throw to be recorded in an epigram, and therefore it is likely to have been a remarkable feat. The throw measured a mere 30 metres (95 feet). The current Olympic record is 67.50 metres (205.74 feet) and as discus-throwing had already been practised for centuries before Phaullus' time, by today's standards this was certainly not a medal-winning performance. The length of the other recorded throw was one of 150 feet (45.72 metres), by the amiable ghost whom we met earlier, which can hardly count, but one would perhaps expect something phenomenal from this superhuman athlete. A possible explanation is that the accepted method of throwing was so stylised as to prevent the athlete from using his full potential for distance. To the Greeks rhythm and grace were of vital importance in athletics; it is known that exercise was often performed to the accompaniment of music and it is more than likely that the discus-thrower attempted to achieve almost a dance movement. The centrifugal force utilised in today's free-style discus-throwing has undoubtedly made possible a dramatic increase in distance.

Javelin-throwing

'*We recommend two Persian javelins of cornel wood. . .and we advise throwing the javelin from as great a distance as possible, for this gives a man more time to turn his horse and to grasp the other javelin. Here are some brief instructions on the most effective method of throwing a javelin. If a man draws back his right side as he advances with the left, rises a little from the thighs and discharges the javelin with its point a little upwards, he will give his weapon the strongest impetus and the furthest carrying power. . .*'
Xenophon, fourth century BC, *On the Art of Horsemanship* XII 12-13

Javelin-throwing, of all athletic events, had the strongest connections with warfare. From Mycenaean times until the Roman Empire, soldiers relied heavily upon the javelin as an offensive weapon. It differed from the spear in that it was lighter and was thrown rather than thrust. It enabled a man to attack the enemy from a distance before engaging in hand-to-hand fighting, and was particularly effective when thrown from horseback, as Xenophon has demonstrated. At some games mounted javelin-throwing at a target was included in the programme, but at Olympia contestants competed on foot.

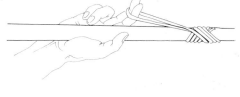

(Left) Mounted riders aim javelins at a target. Although this event was not included in the Olympic Games, it was a popular contest at other festivals.
Panathenaic amphora of the early fourth century BC. BM Reg. no. 1903.2–17.1.

(Below left) Four pentathletes: a jumper, a discus-thrower, and two javelin-throwers. The javelin-thrower on the right merely carries his javelin, while the other is poised ready to throw.
Panathenaic amphora, *c.* 525 BC. BMC Vases B 134.

(Below) The method of holding a javelin by the thong, as used by the javelin-thrower in the scene *below left*. Sometimes the thong was knotted onto the shaft, while at others it was merely twisted round and came free after the throw.

Athletes used javelins which were lighter than the military ones, for their object was distance rather than penetration. These athletic javelins were made of elderwood, while soldiers used a type made from a hard wood like cornel, yew or pine. The athletic javelin was roughly the height of the thrower and it seems that for practice purposes it was often blunt. In a competition the point would probably be sharpened, so that it would stick into the ground, otherwise it would have been difficult to measure the length of the throw.

There was one major difference between the ancient and the modern technique of throwing a javelin: Greek athletes used a leather thong (*ankyle*) which was wound round the middle of the shaft. When the javelin was thrown the thong unwound, having the same effect as the spiral grooves inside a rifle barrel: it made the javelin spin, ensuring a steadier flight. Modern experiments have shown that use of the thong increases the chances of pitching on the point, although it has hardly any effect on distance. We have no detailed information about the length of the throws that were achieved in ancient times, since, in general, there seems to have been little concern about making records, but contemporary writers imply that throws of three hundred feet were possible.

Except for the use of the thong the Greek method of javelin-throwing was identical to ours. The athlete ran up to the mark carrying the javelin in his right hand horizontally at ear-level, brought it back for the throw extending his left arm forward to aid his balance, and then thrust the javelin forward.

The contest took place in the stadium and competitors were required to throw from the same *balbis* (rectangular area) as the discus-throwers used. They were probably allowed three throws, as athletes depicted on pottery often carry three javelins, and furthermore at games on the island of Cos victors were given three javelins as a prize.

Long-jump

Student: *Just now Socrates asked Chairophon how many of its own feet a flea could jump – do you see? – because one of them had just bitten Chairophon's eyebrow and jumped over onto Socrates' head.*
Strepsiades: *Well, how did he find out?*
Student: *He used a most elegant method. He melted some wax and then dipped the flea's feet into it, so that when it was set the flea had a pair of Persian slippers on.*
And then he took them off its feet and measured the distance out, like this, you see. . .(taking a step or two, toe touching heel)
Aristophanes, fifth century BC, *Clouds* 142-50

Aristophanes' audience would often have seen athletes pacing out the length of their jumps to see how well they had done. The flea could not be expected to follow suit and so the obvious solution was to find out his shoe size and use it as a unit of measure.

The long-jump was the only type of jumping contest in Greek athletics. It must be remembered that every event was originally intended as a form of training for warfare; rarely would the crossing of Greek terrain necessitate a high-jump, but it would often demand a leap over a stream or ravine.

In the ancient depictions the only time that we see someone using a pole in the same manner as the modern pole-vaulter is to leap on to a horse, although Homer tells us that the agile Nestor once escaped the charge of the Calydonian Boar by pole-vaulting into a tree with the aid of his hunting-spear.

One glance at a representation of a Greek long-jumper will show the vital difference between the ancient and modern methods. The Greeks always used weights called *halteres*. On take-off they were swung forward with as much force as possible, propelling the jumper forward. As he came down to land he swung them backwards, providing the thrust to achieve those vital extra inches. Philostratus says that the jumper was disqualified unless he made a clean impression in the sand with both feet: modern athletes experimenting with weights have found however that the only way to obtain a clean landing is to cast them away over the shoulders on descent. If they were retained the jumper tended to sit backwards in the sand, and if they were thrown away underarm he tipped forward. No doubt the ancient athlete acquired his skill from constant practice. Even the Greeks regarded it as the most difficult of events, and Philostratus says that is the reason why the pipes were so

This is probably how jumping weights were used.

often played to accompany the jump. Just as today music was often played to accompany exercise. To achieve an outstanding jump, split-second timing was essential in the movement of arms and legs. The value of the music in creating rhythm and encouraging concentration was thought to be more necessary here than in any other contest.

Though we are used to seeing a running start, it is not certain that this method was used in antiquity. The sill in the stadium, which served as a take-off point (*bater*), was only twenty yards from the perimeter. This would not allow enough space for the modern method. The recent trials mentioned above indicated also that the weights were unwieldy in a running leap and that they reduced the length of the jump which was otherwise possible. But again, is it a question of practice? It seems quite possible, to judge from surviving illustrations, that a short run was used, that the jumper started with the weights held close up to his body, ran a short way still holding them to the front, then as he neared the take-off point he swung them back at arm's length and then forward on the moment of take-off.

A number of halteres have survived. Like the discuses they vary in size and weight. The lengths are between 12 and 29 centimetres, the weights between about 1 and 4½ kilograms. They also differ in shape and it is possible to date the periods

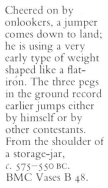

Cheered on by onlookers, a jumper comes down to land; he is using a very early type of weight shaped like a flat-iron. The three pegs in the ground record earlier jumps either by himself or by other contestants. From the shoulder of a storage-jar, *c.* 575–550 BC. BMC Vases B 48.

Two different types of jumping-weight: a pair of flat ones made out of lead (BM reg. no. 1837.6–9.83) and a cylindrical stone type with carved finger grips (BM reg. no. 1867.5–6.48).

when each type was most popular. The earliest ones, in use by the middle of the sixth century BC, are similar in shape to a telephone receiver and made of either stone or metal. Towards the end of the century they were modified: the front end became heavier, and the size and position of the recess for the thumb and fingers indicates that it must have been held further towards the back. The lead and iron examples are usually flat. During the fifth century another type was introduced which was usually made of stone, in the shape of a bar, flat underneath, rounded on top and rounded or pointed at each end. It was held by means of recesses carved out in the sides. After the fifth century it is not certain which type of halter was preferred, but Roman copies of Greek athletic statues usually show a round, cylindrical type with grooves for the fingers.

For us, the greatest problem about the ancient long-jump is in determining whether it was a single, double, or even triple jump. Only two measurements of ancient jumps are now recorded. One was by Phaullos of Croton whom we met earlier as a discus-thrower, and this was 16.28 metres. The other was by Chionis of Sparta who, around the middle of the century, achieved a jump of 16.66 metres. Both these are almost double the current record of 8.90 metres for a single jump, and therefore they have often been rejected as pure fiction on the grounds of sheer physical capability. But they do make sense if we assume that the ancient event was some kind of multiple jump. (The current triple-jump record is 17.39 metres). This appears to be confirmed by a statement in Aristotle's *Physics*, where he says that the jump in the pentathlon is not a single continuous movement. Further, Phaullos' noteworthy jump apparently rewarded him with a broken leg since he landed on hard ground, five feet beyond the end of the *skamma* or sandpit. It would have been scarcely necessary to maintain a fifty-foot pit for jumps which were normally only about one-third of this length.

Combat

The 'heavy' events as the Greeks called them, wrestling, the *pankration* (a kind of all-in wrestling) and boxing, were always big attractions at the Games. But they were more than mere sport and entertainment; they were one of the essential aspects of Greek athletic education. Experience in the martial arts was of paramount importance to the future warrior. Wealthy families could afford to hire a trainer, a *paidotribes*, who is frequently depicted on pottery and gemstones, instructing his pupils with the aid of a cleft stick. With professional tuition unarmed combat became almost an art. Those who could not afford to exercise in the palaistra with a private trainer, practised in the public gymnasium. The Spartans, however, rejected the 'niceties' taught by a professional tutor, and chose instead to rely on sheer power and endurance. One young Spartan composed a boastful epigram on this theme:

'The other wrestlers are stylists. I win by my strength, as is only right and fitting for a Spartan youth'.

Wrestling

'You, throw your arms around him – You, get under his grip. You, push your foot between his and close with him. . .'

From a second-century AD papyrus giving instructions for wrestling drill.

There were basically two types of wrestling: upright or proper wrestling, and ground wrestling. The distinction was in the types of hold that were allowed and the method of deciding the victor. In the first the object was to throw the opponent to the ground. Three falls were necessary to win, and hence the victor became known as the *triakter* or 'trebler'. Touching the ground with the back, shoulders or hip constituted a fall. The contest continued without intervals until one man had thrown his opponent three times. In ground wrestling, victory did not depend on the number of falls but continued until one competitor acknowledged defeat. This was done by raising the right hand with the index finger pointed.

Only the upright type was allowed in wrestling competitions and the pentathlon, but both this and ground wrestling were permitted in the pankration (see p.60). In both versions of wrestling, tripping was allowed but biting and gouging were forbidden (gouging meant digging the fingers into the eyes, mouth or any tender part of the body).

Both sports were allotted their own specific area within the palaistra: upright wrestling usually took place in the *skamma*, a carefully levelled and sanded section of ground, while ground-wrestling was often staged in an area specially watered to make it muddy and sticky, so that it became known as the *keroma* or 'beeswax'.

Like other athletes, wrestlers anointed themselves with olive-oil. Powder was then dusted on to afford the opponent a grip, otherwise it would have been rather like a game of 'catch the greasy pig'. Aristophanes, however, relates how unscrupulous wrestlers would secretly wipe an oily hand over some part of their body which the opponent was likely to grasp. He also tells of a wrestler who was thrown and then hastily rubbed off the sand from his shoulders to remove the evidence of a fall. Wrestlers, like other sportsmen, competed nude, and wore their

(Far left) The end of a contest in the pankration. The victor aims a final blow while the loser raises his right index finger in submission. The man on the right makes sure that the judge has noticed. Greek storage-jar, c. 520–500 BC. BMC Vases 271.

(Left) A wrestling session supervised by a *paidotribes* or trainer. An *aryballos* or oil-flask hangs from the tree. On the left is a *herm*, a pillar surmounted by a bust of Hermes who was the patron god of wrestlers. For this reason herms were often set up in the palaistra and gymnasium. Cast from a Roman sealstone, 14 × 16 mm. BMC Engraved Gems and Cameos 2137.

hair short so that it could not be grasped by their opponent. Some wore a tight-fitting leather cap, such as the Roman poet Martial sent to a friend:

'*So that the duty of the mud-ring may not soil your sleek hair*'.

It seems that up to sixteen competitors took part in a contest; two sets of lots marked with letters of the alphabet were drawn from a helmet or bronze bowl, and the two wrestlers who drew the same letter were required to fight each other. If there was an odd number, as in boxing, one man drew a bye. If there was only one entrant, he would win without having to fight, and if so he was said to win *akonitei*, 'without touching the dust'. On one occasion this happened to Milo, a wrestler from Croton in southern Italy, who lived in the sixth century BC. On his way to receive the crown he had the misfortune to slip and fall on his hip; the crowd jested that he should not win after having had a 'fall'.

Most of our evidence for the holds and tackles employed in Greek wrestling comes from the scenes on pottery, portraying not only real life but also mythological contests between gods, heroes and beasts. The artists could find inspiration for these scenes in their local palaistra or gymnasium.

The illustrations show a variety of tactics. There was no weight distinction in any

(Opposite) The head
of a wrestler wearing
a leather cap to
prevent his opponent
from gripping his
hair.
Etruscan, third
century BC.
Height 20.3 cm.
BMC Bronzes 1614.

of the contests and consequently the biggest men tended to win. To maintain the advantage of weight a high-protein diet of cheese or meat was recommended, although Aristotle warned against over-feeding and also over-training boy athletes. He believed that it made them muscle-bound and lethargic. It seems that few boy athletes went on to win in adult competitions for, of all the boy victors recorded at Olympia, only two went on to win victories in the contests for men.

The greatest wrestler of all time was probably Milo who was mentioned a little earlier. He won five times at Olympia and gained another twenty-five victories at other 'circuit' games. Only when attempting a sixth Olympic victory, when he must have been at least thirty-nine or forty years old, was he finally defeated by a younger man, Timotheos. Milo's popularity, however, was undiminished, and the crowd rushed into the stadium, lifted him onto their shoulders and carried him round, Timotheos cheering along with them.

A demonstration of
the flying mare,
observed by a trainer
or judge.
From a Greek
drinking cup,
c. 450–425 BC.
BMC Vases E 94.

The 'heave'.
A pair of jumping
weights hangs in the
background, with a
strigil and oil-flask to
the left.
From a Greek
drinking cup,
c. 475–450 BC.
BM reg. no.
1928.1–17.59.

59

Many tales were told about Milo. Once he is said to have eaten a whole four-year-old heifer which, earlier the same day, he had carried all round the Altis. On another occasion during the sampling of the new wine at the *Anthesterion* festival, he downed three *choai* (about nine litres) of wine, all for a bet. This amazing character was also reputed to be a disciple of Pythagoras and to have written several treatises. His end was both tragic and ironic. While out in the forest one day he came upon a newly-cut tree trunk with the wedges in place ready for it to be split open. He decided to use his own strength to force it apart. The wedges flew out, but his hands were trapped, and that night he was eaten by wild animals.

Pankration

'Pankratiasts. . .must employ backward falls which are not safe for the wrestler. . .They must have skill in various methods of strangling; they also wrestle with an opponent's ankle and twist his arm, besides hitting and jumping on him, for all these practices belong to the pankration, only biting and gouging being excepted.'

Philostratos, second-third century AD, *On Gymnastics*

It is no surprise that at least one athlete, Sarapion of Alexandria, ran away the day before the pankration because he was afraid of his opponents.

The pankration may seem the most violent of Greek sports to us; the Greeks however considered it less dangerous than boxing. Because it was such a crowd-puller, it was one of the first sports to be taken over by professionals. By the end of the fourth century BC few amateurs entered the contests and at many of the local games the prize-money for the pankration was considerably more than for any other event.

Prizes were given not merely for brute strength, and skill was just as essential as it was in wrestling. Eight of Pindar's odes are in honour of pankratiasts, and they refer to all the qualities which symbolised the contemporary athletic ideal.

Both upright and ground wrestling, which have already been described, were allowed in the pankration. Striking with the fist or open hand was also allowed, and leg- and foot-holds were common. As in ground wrestling, the object was to force

Two pankratiasts struggle on the ground; the man on the right tries to gouge out his opponent's eye, a foul for which the trainer is about to strike him with his cleft stick. Behind hang a discus in a bag and a bundle of boxing thongs. On the left: boxers. From a Greek drinking-cup, *c.* 500–475 BC. BMC Vases E 78.

your opponent to submit, and although gouging and biting were forbidden, scenes on pottery show that pankratiasts often tried to get away with both. Biting was certainly ridiculed, and Plutarch tells how Alkibiades, as a desparate measure to avoid being thrown, bit his opponent's hand; the other released his grip, exclaiming, 'You bite, like a woman, Alkibiades.' 'No', he answered, 'like a lion.' Kicking was also scorned, and in his parody of the Olympic Games, Galen, a Roman physician of the third century AD, awards the prize for the pankration to the donkey since it was the best of all animals at kicking.

At the beginning of a bout contestants usually sparred with their hands and fists, twisting each other's arms and fingers; this was known as *akrocheirismos*. Sostratos, a pankratiast from Sikyon, was famous for breaking his opponent's fingers to gain a submission at the very beginning of the contest. Because of this habit he became known as 'Mr Finger-Tips'. Pausanias disapproved of this trick and says that it was used only by contestants who could not achieve a fall. Most of the struggle took place on the ground, as each of the combatants wished to avoid a heavy fall, and learning to 'wrestle on the knees' was one aspect of a thorough training.

Pankratiasts from different regions had their own specialities. One short cut to victory was the stranglehold, which was greatly favoured by the Eleans, but the ladder-grip, *klimakismos*, was most effective, as admirably demonstrated by Herakles and the Triton. Lucian's *Anacharsis* humorously describes how the enemies of the Greeks would take flight for fear of this hold,

'lest, as they stand gaping, you fill their mouths with sand, or jumping round to get on their backs, twist your legs round their bellies, squeeze your arms beneath their helmets, and strangle them to death'.

A spectacular feat was the stomach-throw, where a man grabbed hold of his opponent, rolled on to his back, planting his foot firmly in the other's stomach, and propelled him clean over his head to a thunderous landing. Referring to such tactics, Pindar likens Melissos to the fox that rolls on her back 'spreads out her feet and deflects the swoop of the eagle'.

As leg - and foot-holds were permitted in the pankration, a man would often

Artists adapted scenes which they saw in the palaistra and gymnasium for mythological battles. Here Herakles uses a ladder-grip on Triton, who was half man, half fish, and a body-lift on the giant Antaios. Greek storage-jar, *c.* 520–500 BC. Height 29.3 cm. BMC Vases B 494.

Bronze coin of Antoninus Pius, from Alexandria. BMC Coins Alexandria 1054.

61

grasp his opponent by the foot, lift it up and tilt him over backwards. A small stocky Cilician athlete, nicknamed 'Jumping Weight', because he was shaped like one, won great renown for his 'heel-trick'. Instead of releasing his opponent's foot after obtaining a fall in this way he would keep hold of it, forcing a submission by twisting it out of its socket.

The most famous Olympic pankratiasts were Theagenes of Thasos and Polydamas of Scotussa. Theagenes won fourteen hundred crowns at various Greek festivals and his strength was reputedly so great that at the age of nine, taking a fancy to a bronze statue in the local market-place, he picked it up and carried it off. In subsequent years his own statue stood at Olympia next to that of Alexander the Great. Amongst other achievements Polydamas strangled a lion with his bare hands, a feat that is depicted on his statue-base, which survives at Olympia. He also stopped a chariot dead in its tracks by seizing hold of it as it sped past him.

Boxing

'Glaukos was originally a farmer. One day the ploughshare came away from the plough and his father observed Glaukos hammering it back with his bare fist. Impressed by his son's great strength, the old man decided to take him to the next Olympic Games. This he did and Glaukos fought his way through to the final of the contest. But he was inexperienced and so took a great deal of punishment in the preliminary bouts. Consequently when he came to face his last opponent he was so badly wounded that everybody thought he would have to give up, but his father called out to him "My boy, remember the ploughshare!" whereupon Glaukos hit his opponent so hard that the contest was ended there and then.'

Pausanias, second century AD, *Description of Greece* VI 10, 1–3

Boxing is a very ancient sport, depicted by artists as early as the Minoan and Mycenaean periods.

The Greeks always liked to embellish time-honoured tradition with divine origins. The god Apollo, who was particularly associated with boxing, is said to have beaten Ares, god of war, in the first ever boxing contest at Olympia. Herakles was also renowned for his boxing skills, but it was the legendary hero Theseus who was credited with its invention, under the guidance of Athena.

More realistically, the origins of boxing were attributed to the Spartans. In early times they were said to have fought without helmets, considering a shield the only manly form of protection. Boxing hardened their faces and taught them to ward off blows to the head. Ironically they usually refrained from taking part in public boxing contests, and the pankration. These contests were decided when a competitor was either knocked insensible or admitted defeat, which would have brought dishonour to a Spartan.

Boxing was especially popular in the east, and during the early years of the Olympic festival most of the champions were Ionian Greeks from Asia Minor and the islands off its coast. Onomastos of Smyrna, victor of Olympia in 688 BC, is said to have formulated the rules for boxing which were adopted at the Olympic Games, and this, comments Philostratos, was 'although he came from effeminate Ionia'. The eastern Greeks were often scorned for being somewhat flabby but in boxing this may have amounted to an asset rather than a liability. The precise nature of the rules can only be the subject of conjecture, based on the surviving illustrations and literary references. It seems that no wrestling or clinching was allowed, but it was permissible to hit a fallen man.

Virtually any type of blow with the hand was allowed, but gouging with the thumb was forbidden. Scenes on pottery show the use of the hook, upper cuts and rabbit punches, and blows with the side and heel of the hand were not uncommon.

Contests often lasted for many hours, and sometimes the boxers agreed to exchange undefended blows in order to end the contest before nightfall. A fight at Nemea between Damoxenos and Kreugas ended in this way, and it exemplifies the violence of ancient boxing. Kreugas struck first with a blow to his opponent's head; Damoxenos rallied, and jabbed Kreugas under the ribs with outstretched fingers, so viciously that the blow pierced his flesh and tore out the entrails; Kreugas died instantly. It is often claimed that boxing became more bloodthirsty in Roman times, but this brutality would be hard to equal. There are surprisingly few

(Right) Philostratos says that a paunch was a useful asset to a boxer because it made it more difficult for his opponent to score a blow to the head. Here the slim athlete on the left stands ready to wrestle, but his corpulent companion, boxing thongs in hand, would clearly prefer fisticuffs. *Right*, a javelin-thrower and a discus-thrower. Greek drinking-cup, *c.* 510–500 BC. Height 14 cm. BMC Vases E 6.

(Left) Two boxers on a fragment of a Mycenaean pot from Cyprus, *c.* 1300–1200 BC. Height 19.6 cm. BMC Vases C 334.

63

references to fatal accidents in boxing during the one thousand years that contests were held. On such occasions the dead man was posthumously awarded the crown and his opponent banished forever from the stadium where the contests were held.

The fights did not take place in a ring, which meant that there was no opportunity for cornering, and at Olympia the boxing events were at midday, so that neither competitor had the sun in his eyes, As in other combat events, lots were drawn beforehand, and if there was an odd number of contestants one man drew a bye, which meant that for the next heat he became an *ephedros* or 'sitter-by'. At the start of the contest, boxers advanced *deinon derkomenoi*, 'looking daggers and meaning business'; there was no bonhomie or shaking of hands.

It is difficult to trace the evolution of the sport, but the development of the glove reflects some of the changes that took place. Until around 500 BC the 'well-cut thongs of ox-hide' recorded by Homer remained standard. These thin strips of leather, ten to twelve feet long, are often depicted hanging in bundles in the palaistra. They were secured to the hand by a loop at each end, and we often see athletes adjusting them before the contest. The thongs were occasionally dressed with oil or fat to keep them supple; although they were known as 'soft' gloves, their purpose was probably to protect the knuckles rather than to avoid injury to an opponent, and boxers are often shown with severe cuts on their faces (see p.60).

This type was used for practice during the fourth century BC, but a new glove was evolved for competitions. These were called *sphairai*, and consisted of a padded inner glove bound on by stiff leather thongs. Binding them on must have been a complicated business, and almost immediately after their introduction the first type of ready-made glove, the 'hard' glove, appears. The most distinctive feature of these was a band formed by several thick strips of stout leather encircling the knuckles, and making a very effective knuckle-duster. The fingers were left free, but the thonging extended well up the forearm. The colloquial name for these gloves was *myrmykes* or 'ants', because of their sting. Often a band of fleece was added round the forearm with which the athlete could wipe off sweat; modern tennis-players use a similar device. These gloves, although formidable, were not nearly as vicious as the Roman *caestus*, which were weighted with iron or lead.

The tactics of ancient boxing were fairly simple. Virtually all blows were directed to the head, while the body was left exposed. The scenes on pottery show that most damage was done to the nose, cheek and chin; it was the pankratiast or wrestler who was more likely to suffer from a cauliflower ear. Fighting techniques were refined over the years, and a century after the introduction of boxing at Olympia, Pythagoras of Samos was said to be the first man to box 'scientifically'. At a later date, when the art of boxing had deteriorated, contestants relied heavily on defensive tactics, and they were trained to keep their arms up for long periods. Melankomas of Caria, an Olympic victor of the first century AD, is reputed to have been able to keep up his guard for two days, and thus, skipping round his opponent without a blow being struck, the other man eventually yielded, from exhaustion and sheer frustration. It is no wonder that Melankomas boasted his face to be as unscarred as that of any runner.

Various other exercises were performed during training. Shadow-fighting, *skiamachia*, was popular, and the famous boxer Glaukos was honoured with a statue

(Right) A boxer
adjusts the thonging
of a 'hard-glove'.
The sheepskin lining
is indicated on the
forearm.
From a panathenaic
amphora, 336 BC.
BMC Vases B 607.

(Far right) Two
African boxers, one
staggering back from
an upper-cut.
Second or first
century BC,
Height 26.3 cm
and 24.4 cm.
BMC Terracottas
D 84 and D 85.

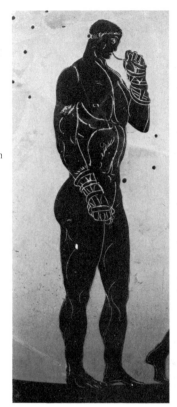

which represented him in this attitude. The medical writer Antyllus recommended that:

'The shadow-boxer must not only use his hands but also his legs, sometimes as if he were jumping, at other times as if he were kicking'.

Footwork was of course very important: Statius describes how Alkidamas defeated his heavier opponent Kapaneos by avoiding 'a thousand deaths that flit around his temples by quick movement and by the help of his feet'.

Attacking the punch-ball or *korykos* was another common exercise; Antyllus proposed that stronger men should have it filled with sand and weaker men with millet or flour. Another effective way to strengthen the muscles was to break up hard ground with a pick, an activity which was necessary to provide a pitch, or *skamma*, for a contest. This type of exertion was so popular among boxers that the pick, or *skapane*, came to be recognised as their symbol (see p.34).

The most renowned boxer in ancient times was Diagoras of Rhodes, who was of royal descent, and was said to be the tallest man that ever lived. He won once at Olympia (464 BC) twice at Nemea and four times at the Isthmus. He was known as *euthymaches*, the 'fair boxer'. In 448 BC he had the great pleasure of seeing his two sons crowned in the Altis for the pankration and boxing. The boys, overjoyed, lifted him on to their shoulders, and put both wreaths on his head. One of the crowd shouted not out of malice but wonder at this ultimate achievement, 'Die now Diagoras; there is nothing left for you but to rise to Olympos.' And there in his glory Diagoras collapsed and died.

Equestrian events

Chariot-races

'. . .then, at the sound of the bronze trumpet, off they started, all shouting to their horses and urging them on with the reins. The clatter of the rattling chariots filled the whole arena, and the dust flew up as they sped along in a dense mass, each driver goading his team unmercifully in his efforts to draw clear of the rival axles and panting steeds, whose steaming breath and sweat drenched every bending back and flying wheel together.'
Sophokles, fifth century BC, *Elektra* 698–760

This stirring description of a chariot-race shows why this spectacular event remained so popular throughout antiquity.

The earliest literary record of a chariot-race is found in the description of the funeral games in Homer's *Iliad*. Chariot-racing, more than any other event, became associated with the passing of the dead into *Hades*, the Underworld. Only the wealthy aristocrat could afford to equip and maintain a chariot and horses for war or hunting, and to enable him to continue this noble pursuit in the after-life, his chariot and team of horses were often buried or cremated along with him. Excavations have shown that this took place as early as the Mycenaean period.

As noted earlier, athletic festivals probably had their origins in the funeral games held for local heroes. Pelops was the hero of Olympia, and his sanctuary in the Altis was called the Pelopion. It was here during the course of each Olympic festival that rites which included the sacrifice of a black ram were performed in his honour. In mythology Pelops was closely associated with chariot-racing and entered one of the first races to be held at Olympia.

The legendary origin of the equestrian events at Olympia

Oinomaos was King of Pisa, a district not far from Elis, and had a daughter of marriageable age called Hippodameia. Prospective suitors for her hand were required to drive away with her in a chariot. It was agreed that Oinomaos would follow in another chariot, and spear the suitor if he caught up with them. His horses were so swift that the king always succeeded in catching them, and he celebrated his victories by nailing the heads of his unfortunate victims above the palace gateway. The score was twelve when the young Pelops arrived from Phrygia (see p.9).

There are two alternative versions of what happened next. In the first version Pelops bribed Myrtilos, the royal charioteer, to replace the bronze axle-pins of the king's chariot with wax ones, with the result that Oinomaos was thrown to the ground. He was able to do this because Myrtilos was secretly in love with Hippodameia, but was afraid to challenge her father. Pelops promised him a night with Hippodameia as a reward for his help, but after the victory he showed his gratitude by pitching Myrtilos over a cliff into the sea. (It was not necessary for a Greek hero to be virtuous but only to have superhuman strength and cunning.) In the second version Poseidon gave Pelops a golden chariot with four winged horses, and in addition caused the wheels to fly off Oinomaos' chariot, so that he was thrown to his death. At the same time the king's palace was struck by lightning and reduced to ashes, save for one wooden pillar that was revered in the Altis for

(*Above*) 'Make sure your left-hand horse keeps hard by the turning post . . .' So Nestor advised his son before a chariot-race in the Iliad. The long white robes of the charioteer were traditional dress. Panathenaic amphora, *c.* 420–400 BC. BMC Vases 606.

(*Right*) Poseidon was lord of the sea, but here the horse's head in his right hand identifies him in another capacity, as patron god of horses. Charioteers and jockeys would offer prayers and sacrifices to him before competing. Roman bronze statuette. Height 16.9 cm. BMC Bronzes 960.

centuries, and stood near what was to be the site of the Temple of Zeus.

Although the pillar was seen by Pausanias it has long since perished, and excavations have not revealed any trace of the palace foundations. It is possible that the pillar was not really part of a building but the finishing post for races that were originally run towards the heart of the sacred grove. This theory is supported by a curious instance of 'accidental archaeology' in Roman times. Pausanias records that a Roman senator, while digging the foundations for the base of his statue near Oinomaos' pillar, came across fragments of arms, bits and bridles. These may have been the offerings of the earliest victors in the races, for it was the custom in later years for victors to set up dedications of bronze trappings on the banks of the stadium. A number of these offerings have been found in recent excavations, along with inscriptions recording the name of the donor.

Types of event

The chariot-races were of two types: the *tethrippon* for teams of four horses and the *synoris* for teams of two. Both of these were divided into two separate contests, one for horses of any age, the other for colts. At the *dokimasia*, or inspection, before the Games, the judges had to settle any disputes concerning classification into the two groups. On one occasion they disqualified a team entered for the colts' race by a Spartan called Lykinos, because one of the horses was over age, whereupon Lykinos entered his team for the open chariot-race, and won. All the races were of gruelling length, ranging from about two and a half miles for the colts' synoris to over eight miles for the open tethrhippon.

Despite its relatively late introduction, the synoris is likely to have been the oldest type of equestrian event, as it appears on some of the earliest pottery. At Olympia, however, the four-horse chariot-race was the first to be introduced, in 680 BC, while the synoris was eventually recognised as an official event in 408 BC, perhaps due to the increasing importance of cavalry fighting at that time.

A Roman bronze model of a two-horse chariot, of which only one horse remains. Height 18.6 cm. BMC Bronzes 2695.

Thrills and spills

The most hazardous part of the course was undoubtedly the turn. It was crucial to be ahead at the turn, as Nestor advised his son in the *Iliad*; once this was rounded and you were ahead, no-one could touch you. But not everyone was lucky, and Sophokles records what must have been a disastrously familiar occurrence:

At each turn of the lap, Orestes reined in his inner trace-horse and gave the outer its head, so skilfully that his hub just cleared the post by a hair's breadth every time; and so the poor fellow had safely rounded every lap but one without mishap to himself or his chariot. But at the last he misjudged the turn, slackened his left rein before the horse was safely round the bend, and so struck the post. The hub was smashed across, and he was hurled over the rail entangled in the reins, and as he fell his horses ran wild across the course.

Sophokles, fifth century BC, *Elektra* 698-760

Just before the chariots reached the turning post, they had to pass the Taraxippos, or 'horse-terroriser'. This was a circular altar at the edge of the south bank which Pausanias says struck panic into the horses and caused many a disaster. He records many local legends to explain the phenomenon but since other hippodromes had similar features (though none as terrifying as that at Olympia, says Pausanias), a more rational explanation seems necessary. One modern suggestion is that since the equestrian events began at sunrise, then, as the chariots sped along the southern track both horses and drivers would have had the sun directly in their eyes. At the altar, which was situated just before the turn, the tension and bewilderment would be at a climax. The situation of the altar itself was therefore purely coincidental.

The chariots

The chariots themselves appear to have been of such slender construction, without springing, that it is easy to imagine how continual bumping over rutted ground would jar every bone in the driver's body. The four-horse racing-chariot was an

Harnessing-up. The collar for the trace-horse hangs down on this side. From a water-jar, *c.* 520—500 BC. BMC Vases B 304.

adaptation of the Homeric two-horse war-chariot, but lighter, to increase speed, and smaller, as it carried only one person. The middle pair of horses (*zygioi*) were harnessed to a yoke, which was fastened to the pole, and secured by a strap to the rim of the chariot. The outer pair of horses were trace-horses (*seiraphoroi*). The charioteer carried a whip or a goad, sometimes together with a long stick with metal jingles on the end and the horses were controlled by reins and bits, or alternatively nose-bands. The two-horse chariot was generally similar to the four-horse, although the Athenians used a variation, consisting merely of a seat for the driver with an open framework at the back and sides, and a footboard suspended from the pole. This was the same type of chariot that was used for the mule-cart race (see p.71). The chariots were usually made of wood, wickerwork (probably brightly painted), and leather thonging, and were sometimes decorated with sheet-bronze cladding and finials, occasionally inlaid with silver.

A wrecked chariot with the driver on all fours. Cast from an Etruscan carnelian sealstone, *c.* 450–425 BC. 14 × 11 mm. BMC Engraved Gems and Cameos 678.

The charioteers

At the athletic festivals the charioteers were rarely the owners of their chariot and teams. They were usually employed in much the same way as racehorse owners now employ jockeys. Chariot-driving was an extremely hazardous affair, and unless you were a particular devotee of the sport it was not worth risking your own life. In the case of victory, the owner still received all the glory, including the crown, while the driver had to be content with the victory ribbon. In exceptional circumstances the charioteer might be celebrated along with the owner in an ode specially commissioned for the occasion, or he might even be represented in the victory monument. It was considered very honourable to drive your own team, and in one of his odes Pindar congratulates Herodotos of Thebes for doing this. In the fifth century BC Damonon of Sparta boasted in an inscription that he and his son Enymakratidas had won a total of sixty-eight victories in chariot- and horse-races at eight different festivals.

(Above) A figure of Victory personified flies down to crown the victor in a four-horse chariot-race. Below is a panoply or set of armour – a shield, breast-plate, greaves and crested helmet – which was probably the prize at these particular games. Silver coin from Syracuse, fourth century BC. BMC Coins, Syracuse 176.

(Left) A miniature bronze chariot-wheel, dedicated to Zeus. Modest offerings like these are likely to have been made by charioteers rather than by owners of teams. This one, similar to several from Olympia, was dedicated by a certain Eudamas and probably commemorates a victory in the Games at Nemea, where it was found. Fifth century BC. Diameter 10.1 cm. BMC Bronzes 253.

Sponsorship and propaganda

Sometimes chariot entries were financed not by individuals but by states – in 472 BC, for example, the 'public chariot' of the Argives won an Olympic victory. The investment was propaganda, and good publicity for a state which specialised in horse-breeding. Sponsorship and advertisement at equestrian events are really nothing new. The extensive plains of Argos, Euboea, and Thessaly and the area around Athens were renowned for their breeds of horses, but most famous of all were those of Sicily and southern Italy. In those parts, horse-sports were the passionate love of the local princes. They tried to gain popularity and influence with the crowds at major festivals by entering teams of horses in the Games and making numerous dedications. The well-known bronze charioteer of Delphi was part of a chariot-group dedicated by a Syracusan tyrant, probably soon after 474 BC.

To ensure victory it was not unusual for an individual to enter a number of chariots in one race. In 416 BC the Athenian statesman Alkibiades entered seven chariots at the Olympic Games, taking first, second and either third or fourth place. Aristophanes could easily have had him in mind when he ridiculed the fashionable young Athenians who spent vast sums on horses, affected horsey names, and spoke of virtually nothing but horses all day. Alkibiades' enemies levelled all kinds of charges against him, including one of taking a fellow-competitor's horses. At the time he was seeking generalship in a proposed invasion of Sicily, and retaliated strongly, claiming that whereas the Greeks had thought Athens to be weakened by the Peloponnesian War, they now exaggerated her power because of his exceptional performance at the Olympic Games. Political propaganda is by no means peculiar to the modern Olympics.

Alkibiades was not the only Athenian general addicted to chariot-racing. Cimon, the father of the great Miltiades, won the four-horse chariot-race at three successive Olympic Games, in 532, 528 and 524 BC. His horses were honoured not only with bronze statues but with burial in the family tomb.

The most infamous competitor of all was the emperor Nero. He postponed the Games from AD 65 to AD 67, so that he could compete in them during a visit to Greece. He appeared with a ten-horse team, only to be thrown from his chariot. Although he was helped to remount, he failed to finish, but even so, he was proclaimed victor, on the grounds that he would have won had he been able to complete the course. After his death in AD 68, these Games were declared invalid, and Nero's name was expunged from the victor-lists. His successor Galba also insisted that a 250,000 drachma bribe to the judges should be paid back.

The mule-cart race

A silver coin minted for a victory in the mule-cart race at Olympia by Anaxilas of Rhegium. The high, box like seat was peculiar to mule-carts. 484/480 BC. BM reg. no. 1946.1–1. 1090.

The Eleans apparently did not approve of the introduction of this race, known as the *apene*, and it lasted for only fourteen Olympiads. The influential Greeks from Sicily were probably responsible for this innovation at Olympia, as that country was famous for its mules. The event is often depicted on Sicilian coins and several Sicilian mule-cart race winners were celebrated in the Odes of Pindar. In Elis, however, there was an ancient curse on mules bred within the territory, and in view of the religious conservatism of the Games the Eleans would possibly have frowned upon such an event and might have outlawed it at the first opportunity.

Two small jockeys brandish whips to their mounts. Panathenaic amphora, *c.* 480 BC. BMC Vases B 133.

A jubilant young victor in a horse-race. A groom holds up the crown for all to see and bears away on his head the prize, a high-handled tripod. The remains of many similar tripods were found during the excavations of the stadium banks at Olympia, and it is likely that these were prizes at the very early festivals and were subsequently set up by the victors as dedications. A herald walks before the horse proclaiming the victor: 'The horse of Dusnikeitos wins.' Storage jar, *c.* 520–500 BC. BMC Vases B 144.

A victor in the *anabates* race leaps down from his horse. The action is telescoped, for the rider would have dismounted some distance before the finishing post; here a figure of Victory personified holds out the winner's crown. A *krater* or bowl for mixing wine, made in Lucania, Southern Italy, *c.* 400–375 BC. Height 33.3 cm. BM reg. no. 1978.6–15.1.

A silver coin of
Philip II of Macedon
commemorating a
victory in the horse-
race. The rider holds
a palm branch and
the wreath is
depicted beneath his
high-stepping horse.
BM reg. no.
1866.12–1. 1028.

The horse-races

*'The mare of Pheidolas the Corinthian was called ... Aura and, although her rider was
thrown at the beginning of the race, she ran straight on and turned at the pillar; when she
heard the sound of the trumpet, she ran on all the faster and beat the other horses. The Eleans
proclaimed Pheidolas the victor, and allowed him to dedicate this statue of the mare.'*
Pausanias, second century AD, *Description of Greece* VI 13.9

From this story one might imagine that the horse which won at Olympia received
as much adulation as our Derby winner.

Horse-racing in antiquity was just as exciting and even more dangerous than it is
today. The jockeys rode bare-back and without stirrups – these and the saddle had
not yet been invented; moreover at the Olympic festival the horse-races took place
after the chariot events, so that the ground was already well churned and rutted.
One ancient writer claimed that for many people the greatest thrills in horse-racing
were provided by the mishaps that befell the competitors, and it is unlikely that they
were often disappointed. Galen was only too familiar with the consequences of hard
riding which included injuries to the chest, the kidneys and reproductive organs...
'to say nothing of the stumbling of the horses, which has often pitched riders from
their seat, instantly killing them'.

It should be no surprise to learn that jockeys, like charioteers, were usually paid
servants. Some owners did compete themselves and, after all, horse-sports were an
ancient and aristocratic pastime. Military leaders in particular tended to be expert
horsemen. Themistocles taught his sons to ride, throw javelins standing on horseback, and perform other dangerous feats. We have already heard Aristophanes'
criticism of 'horsey' young men, and a passionate interest in racing is confirmed by
the price paid for a race-horse in 421 BC – 1200 drachmai, at least three times the
average annual wage. For the wealthy young man in antiquity a fast horse was just
as essential as today's fast car.

Types of race

The ordinary horse-race was run over six stades, a little under 1200 metres. There
were also two other equestrian events at Olympia. These were a race for colts, and
another for mares, called the *calpe* or *anabates* ('dismounter'). In the latter the rider
dismounted for the last stretch and ran beside his horse. Its origins were probably
military since speed and agility were essential for a horseman in battle. It is
interesting that a similar event is included in our gymkhanas.

An *anabates* depicted on a silver coin from Tarentum.
Although the event was a late introduction at Olympia,
representations of various dates from Sicily and Southern
Italy prove that it had a long and popular history there.
Third century BC. Diameter 85 mm. BMC Coins.
Tarentum 255.

7 Prizegiving

The greatest achievement for an athlete in the ancient world was to win the Olympic crown. The material prizes offered at other athletic festivals were insignificant compared to the fame and glory earned by the Olympic victor.

The sacred olive-tree (Plan 5) from which the wreaths were made stood amid a cluster to the rear of the Temple of Zeus. King Iphitos of Elis had offered a wreath as a prize on the instruction of the Delphic Oracle, which told him to go to Olympia and search for the tree decked in gossamer webs (cobwebs were considered to be a sign of rain and they were therefore connected with fertility). Iphitos returned to Olympia, found the tree, and encircled it with a fence. It came to be known as the *kotinos kallistephanos*, 'the olive beautiful for its crowns'. According to Aristotle it was remarkable because its leaves grew in a symmetrical pattern like the myrtle, and because, unlike other olives, the leaves were pale green on the upper side and not, as is usual, on the underside. Before each festival it was the custom for a young boy whose parents were still alive to cut the branches with a golden sickle. One branch was cut for each contest so that the victor's crown could be made from it.

It is uncertain where and when the crowning took place. There is evidence for

A winner is presented with tokens of victory: palm branches and fillets, or woollen ribbons, which were tied round the head, arms or legs.
From a Greek drinking-cup, about 500–475 BC.
BMC Vases E 52.

two different ceremonies held at different stages in the history of the Games. According to one account the victors were crowned immediately after the competition. This must have been the practice in later times for when in AD 107 the boxer Apollonios arrived late for his contest, he found that he had been disqualified and the crown was already in place on the head of his opponent Herakleides. Enraged, he bound on his boxing thongs and started a vicious attack on him.

Pausanias records that, in the Temple of Hera, there was a gold and ivory table designed by Kolotes, a pupil of Pheidias, on which the wreaths for the victors were displayed. The table may have been taken to the stadium for the prizegiving ceremony; there would have been ample space for it in front of the seats on the judges' stand.

According to another version, which has been adopted for our programme, the victors were not crowned until a special ceremony at the end of the festival, held in front of the statue in the Temple of Zeus. In the meantime ribbons of wool were tied around the athlete's head, arms and legs as a mark of victory and at a later date he was also given a palm branch.

Marble statue of a young athlete binding on a victor's ribbon.
Roman copy of a Greek bronze original of about 440 BC.
Height 1.38 m. BMC Sculpture 501.

8 Celebrations

'. . . .and the whole company raised a great cheer, while the lovely light of the fair-faced moon lit up the evening. Then, in joyful celebration, the whole Altis rang with banquet-song.'
Pindar, fifth century BC, *Olympian Odes* x 73-8

In addition to the public banquet for victors there were various private celebrations in the evenings. The wine flowed, and there was song and revelry. Victors and friends alike decked themselves in garlands and processed round the Altis singing victory hymns, which were either time-honoured chants or odes specially composed for the occasion by leading poets such as Pindar or Bacchylides. The wealthier the victor the larger and more luxurious the celebration. Both Alkibiades of Athens and Anaxilas of Rhegion provided magnificent feasts to celebrate their victories. Empedokles of Agrigentum was a disciple of Pythagoras and accordingly a vegetarian. He made an ox of dough, mixed with incense and garnished with costly herbs and spices, and distributed it among the spectators. Often the party continued all night, and on the following morning the victors (who one hopes were not competing again that day) made solemn vows and sacrifices to the appropriate gods.

Homeward-bound

After the feasting on the final day there remained the problem of getting home. One is reminded of the present day chaos after a football match when Lucian complains that he could not get a carriage 'because too many people were departing at the same time'.

Although the Games had come to an end, the fame of the victor lived on. His statue was erected in the Altis, provided of course that he could afford it himself, or

(Left) Five youths, dancing to the music of the double pipes and filling their drinking-cups with wine from a mixing-bowl or krater. From a Greek drinking-cup, *c.* 500–475 BC. Height 10.1 cm. BMC Vases E 37.

it was paid for by his friends, relations or the state. Hundreds of these statues were dedicated but now after the ravages of time, very little remains except bases and small fragments. Were it not for Pausanias, we would know very little about this vast open-air art gallery.

An athlete might also be commemorated by a statue set up in his home-town. In addition he would often be allowed to dine for life at public expense, he would be given sums of money and was granted civic honours. On his return from the Games he was given a civic reception followed by further feasting and celebrations. Exainetos of Akragas in Sicily, who won the stade race for a second time in 420 BC, was escorted in procession by three hundred chariots drawn by white horses.

Formal and informal celebrations.

(*Above*) Boys serve wine to reclining banqueters; jugs and drinking-cups hang on the wall behind. From a Greek drinking-cup, *c.* 500–475 BC. Height 12.8 cm. BMC Vases E 49.

(*Right*) An inscription on a stone slab commemorating the achievements of a Roman athlete named Lucius who 'won at the Didymaean Games, competed for the crown at Olympia, and competed in all the other athletic festivals in a manner worthy of victory'. Height 80 cm. BMC Inscriptions 928.

77

9 The End of the Ancient Olympic Games

The Games were introduced as a religious ceremony in honour of Zeus, but as time went by belief in the traditional religion faded, and the Games lost their religious significance. The ideology behind the Games reached its zenith in the fifth century BC. During this period the neutrality of the Eleans ensured their control of the festival. In the course of the Peloponnesian War the Eleans abandoned their neutrality and sided with the Athenians, banning the Spartans from the Games. Subsequently, in 424 BC under threat of invasion by the Spartans, the Games were held under the protection of thousands of armed troops. The invasion did not in fact take place, but the precautions which had been considered necessary indicated that the authority of the Sacred Truce was on the wane. The religious and nationalistic unity of the Greeks was disintegrating.

In 365 BC the Arcadians, aided by the Pisatans, the old enemies of Elis, seized control of Olympia and occupied the sanctuary. In the following year, when the Arcadians and the Pisatans staged the Games, the Eleans tried unsuccessfully to regain the sanctuary by force. During the siege the forces occupying the Altis plundered the temples in order to pay their mercenaries. Power was restored to the Eleans only when it was feared that the wrath of the gods would be incurred. Although the sanctity of the Olympic Games was preserved for a little longer, men were beginning to usurp the sovereignty of the gods; the athletes credited themselves and not Zeus with their victories. When the Philippeion was constructed in 336 BC, it was adorned with gold and ivory statues of Alexander the Great and his family; previously these materials had been reserved for statues of the gods. In later years the Romans converted the Temple of Meter into a shrine in honour of Rome and the 'divine Augustus'. Two centuries separated these two events, during which time Rome had incorporated the Greek mainland into her empire, and internal strife between Roman political parties took its toll of Greek culture. The Altis suffered most damage at the hands of the Roman general Sulla, who sacked not only Olympia, but also Delphi and Epidauros to finance his wars against the Persian king Mithridates. In order to celebrate the successful conclusion of the war he transferred the Olympic Games to Rome in 80 BC. Following his death two years later, however, the festival was returned to its proper site. For a time the Games took on a new lease of life; Roman interest in sport, and money invested in ostentatious monuments in the sanctuary, helped it to regain its old prestige, but this did not prevent Caligula from trying to have Zeus's gold and ivory statue removed to Rome.

Henceforth it was almost as if the gods had deserted Olympia, and its fortunes declined. In AD 267, the Heruli, a tribe from Southern Russia, invaded the Peloponnese, and the Eleans tried to save the most sacred part of the Altis. They hastily built a wall to enclose the area between the temple of Zeus and the

Bouleuterion, robbing stone from the buildings on the edge of the sanctuary to complete it. Although the Games continued to be held, the sanctuary was never restored to its previous grandeur. It is not certain when the last festival was celebrated. It has been suggested that it was not staged later than AD 393, because at that time Theodosius I, the first Christian Emperor of Rome, banned all pagan cults. On the other hand they may have continued until the Temple of Zeus was burnt down in approximately AD 426, possibly in accordance with the edict of Theodosius II who ordered all pagan temples in the eastern Mediterranean to be destroyed. Between the fifth and eighth centuries AD successive waves of invaders, – Visigoths, Avars, Vandals and Slavs – laid waste to the Altis, which in time was totally devastated by earthquakes, floods and landslides. It was to be another thousand years before archaeologists excavated the fertile ground of Olympia and replanted in men's minds the seeds of the Olympic ideal.

(Right) A winged figure representing Victory crowns an athlete with an olive-wreath; in his hand is an olive branch. Cast from a sealstone of the second or first century BC. 23 × 16 mm. BMC Engraved Gems and Cameos 1198.

'If the Olympic Games were being held now...you would be able to see for yourself why we attach such great importance to athletics. No-one can describe in mere words the extraordinary... pleasure derived from them and which you yourself would enjoy if you were seated among the spectators feasting your eyes on the prowess and stamina of the athletes, the beauty and power of their bodies, their incredible dexterity and skill, their invincible strength, their courage, ambition, endurance and tenacity. You would never stop...applauding them.'

Lucian, second century AD, *Anacharsis* 12.

Further Reading

Ludwig Drees, *Olympia: Gods, Artists and Athletes*, English translation, Pall Mall Press, 1968.

A.Mallwitz, *Olympia und seine Bauten*, Prestel Verlag München, 1972.

H.-V.Hermann, *Olympia: Heiligtum und Wettkampfstätte*, Hirmer Verlag München, 1972.

E.Norman Gardiner, *Olympia, Its History and Remains*, Clarendon Press, 1925

E.Norman Gardiner, *Athletics of the Ancient World*, Clarendon Press, 1930, reprinted Ares Publishers Inc. Chicago, 1978.

E.Norman Gardiner, *Greek Athletic Sports and Festivals*, Macmillan, 1910.

M.I.Finley and H.W.Pleket, *The Olympic Games: the First Thousand Years*, Chatto & Windus, 1976.

H.A.Harris, *Greek Athletes and Athletics*, Hutchinson, 1964.

H.A.Harris, *Sport in Greece and Rome*, Thames & Hudson, 1972.